SCHAUM'S™
EASY OUTLINES

German

Online Diagnostic Test

Go to **Schaums.com** to launch the Schaum's Diagnostic Test.

This convenient application provides a 30-question test that will pinpoint areas of strength and weakness to help you focus your study. Questions cover all aspects of German grammar covered by this book. With a question-bank that rotates daily, the Schaum's Online Test also allows you to check your progress and readiness for final exams.

Other titles featured in Schaum's Online Diagnostic Test:

Schaum's Easy Outlines: Spanish, 2nd Edition
Schaum's Easy Outlines: French, 2nd Edition
Schaum's Easy Outlines: Italian, 2nd Edition
Schaum's Easy Outlines: Writing and Grammar, 2nd Edition
Schaum's Easy Outlines: Calculus, 2nd Edition
Schaum's Easy Outlines: Geometry, 2nd Edition
Schaum's Easy Outlines: Statistics, 2nd Edition
Schaum's Easy Outlines: College Algebra, 2nd Edition
Schaum's Easy Outlines: Biology, 2nd Edition
Schaum's Easy Outlines: Human Anatomy and Physiology, 2nd Edition
Schaum's Easy Outlines: Beginning Chemistry, 2nd Edition
Schaum's Easy Outlines: Organic Chemistry, 2nd Edition
Schaum's Easy Outlines: College Chemistry, 2nd Edition

SCHAUM'S™
EASY OUTLINES

German

Second Edition

Elke Gschossman-Hendershot
Lois M. Feuerle
Edda Weiss
Conrad J. Schmitt

Abridgement Editor:
Sigmund J. Barber

McGraw Hill

New York   Chicago   San Francisco   Lisbon   London   Madrid   Mexico City
Milan   New Delhi   San Juan   Seoul   Singapore   Sydney   Toronto

The McGraw·Hill Companies

Copyright © 2011 by The McGraw-Hill Companies, Inc. All rights reserved. Printed in the United States of America. Except as permitted under the United States Copyright Act of 1976, no part of this publication may be reproduced or distributed in any form or by any means, or stored in a database or retrieval system, without the prior written permission of the publisher.

1 2 3 4 5 6 7 8 9 10 11 12 13 14 15   DOC/DOC   1 9 8 7 6 5 4 3 2 1

ISBN   978-0-07-176058-4
MHID   0-07-176058-X

Library of Congress Cataloging-in-Publication Data

Gschossmann-Hendershot, Elke.
     Schaum's easy outline of German / Elke Gschossmann-Hendershot...[et al.]. — 2nd ed.
          p.   cm. — (Schaum's easy outline)
     Includes index.
     ISBN 0-07-176058-X (alk. paper)
          1. German language—Grammar—Outlines, syllabi, etc.   2. German language—Vocabulary—Outlines, syllabi, etc.   I. Title.   II. Title: Easy outline of German.

PF3118.G78   2010
438.2'421—dc22   2010039823

Trademarks: McGraw-Hill, the McGraw-Hill Publishing logo, Schaum's Easy Outlines, and related trade dress are trademarks or registered trademarks of The McGraw-Hill Companies and/or its affiliates in the United States and other countries and may not be used without written permission. All other trademarks are the property of their respective owners. The McGraw-Hill Companies is not associated with any product or vendor mentioned in this book.

McGraw-Hill books are available at special quantity discounts to use as premiums and sales promotions or for use in corporate training programs. To contact a representative, please e-mail us at bulksales@mcgraw-hill.com.

This book is printed on acid-free paper.

Contents

Chapter 1
THE SOUNDS OF GERMAN:
A KEY TO GERMAN PRONUNCIATION

IN THIS CHAPTER:

✔ *The German Alphabet*
✔ *Basic Pronunciation*
✔ *Word Stress*

German pronunciation is quite phonetic and regular; an understanding of the basic sounds and stress patterns will enable the student to pronounce most words correctly.

The German Alphabet

The German alphabet has the twenty-six standard letters found in the English alphabet plus four letters that are specific to German.

Letter	German Name	Letter	German Name
a	ah	p	peh
b	beh	q	kuh
c	tseh	r	err
d	deh	s	ess

1

e	eh	t	teh
f	eff	u	uh
g	geh	v	fau
h	hah	w	veh
i	ih	x	iks
j	yot	y	üppsilon
k	kah	z	tsett
l	ell	ä	äh (a-umlaut)
m	emm	ö	öh (o-umlaut)
n	enn	ü	üh (u-umlaut)
o	oh	ß	ess-tsett (scharfes ess)

Basic Pronunciation

The pronunciations given below are only approximations; *they are not exact equivalents*. It is essential to avail yourself of every possible opportunity to hear and use spoken German: audiotapes, radio, television, native speakers, etc.

The Vowels

Vowels in German are either long (stressed) or short (unstressed). In our pronunciation key long vowels are followed by a colon, and short vowels stand alone.

Vowel Sound	Examples	Approximate English Sounds
[a]	wann, kalt, ab	w*a*nder
[a:]	ja, Jahr, sagen	f*a*ther
[e]	Bett, Geld, es	m*e*n
[e:]	See, dem, Regen	m*ay*
[i]	immer, ist, nicht	*i*n
[i:]	ihm, Liebe, mir	b*ee*t
[o]	offen, oft, morgen	n*o*t
[o:]	Boot, ohne, wo	s*o*
[u]	Mutter, null, und	f*oo*t
[u:]	Kuh, Stuhl, gut	m*oo*t

[ä]	Männer, Hände	m<u>e</u>n
[ä:]	spät, Käse, Diät	m<u>ay</u>
[ö]	Löffel, können	No close equivalent in English. Approximate the sound by saying *[eh]*, but with rounded lips
[ö:]	schön, böse, Möbel	No close equivalent in English. Pronounce as with *[ö]* above, but draw it out longer
[ü]	müssen, hütte, fünf	No close equivalent in English. Approximate the sound by saying *[i]*, but with rounded lips
[ü:]	Tür, kühl, Ph<u>y</u>sik	No close equivalent in English. Approximate the sound by saying *[i:]*, but with rounded lips

Note : **r** after vowels (**Tü<u>r</u>, wi<u>r</u>, nu<u>r</u>**) and in the often encountered ending -er (**Finger, Fenster, Feuer**) is pronounced like the [a] in sof<u>a</u>.

You Need to Know
The Diphthongs

A diphthong is a combination of two vowel sounds pronounced with a glide. There are three common diphthongs in German.

Diphthong	Examples	Approximate English Sounds
[au]	<u>au</u>f, H<u>au</u>s, Fr<u>au</u>	h<u>ou</u>se
[ei]	<u>ei</u>n, M<u>ai</u>, M<u>ey</u>er	s<u>i</u>te
[eu]	F<u>eu</u>er, h<u>eu</u>te, n<u>eu</u>	n<u>oi</u>se

The Consonants

Many of the German consonants are pronounced more or less as they are in English. Here are some of the differences:

When **b, d, g** appear at the end of a word or syllable, or before **t** or **st,** they are pronounced as **p, t, k:**

> **lieb, liebst, Obst** —> the **b** is pronounced [p]
> **Bad, abends, Schmidt** —> **d** is pronounced [t]
> **Tag, mag, liegt, liegst** —> **g** is pronounced [k]

The consonant cluster **ch** can represent two closely related but different sounds that are not present in English. When **ch** follows the vowels **a, o,** u and the diphthong **au,** it is pronounced toward the back in the throat, with the tongue and mouth in more or less the same position as for the k sound. However, the stream of breath is not cut off as when pronouncing **k,** but is forced through the narrow opening between the tongue and the roof of the mouth. It is very similar to the **ch** in the Scottish word *Loch.*

> **ach, Nacht, Woche, Tochter, Buch, auch**

After the vowels **e, i, ä, ö, ü** and the diphthongs **ei (ai, ay, ey)** and **eu (äu)** and the consonants **l, n, r,** the stream of air is forced through a flatter but wider opening between the tongue and the roof of the mouth which is also pronounced more toward the front of the mouth.

> **schlecht, ich, lächeln, möchte, Bücher, Eiche, euch, welche, München, Kirche**

The German **l** sound is pronounced to the front of the mouth with the tongue flatter and touching the back of the front teeth, producing a much lighter **l** sound than in English, which is pronounced far back in the mouth.

German most commonly uses the uvular **r** (the uvula is the small flap of skin hanging from the soft palate at the back of the mouth)

The consonants **j, w, z** are pronounced as **y, v, ts:**

> **ja, Jahr, Jacke, Juli** —> the **j** is pronounced [y]
> **Wild, Winter, Woche** —> the **w** is pronounced [v]

Zimmer, duzen, Arzt —> the **z** is pronounced [ts]

When an **s** is in initial position preceding a vowel or it stands between two vowels, it is pronounced like an English **z**. In other positions it is usually pronounced like the English **s**.

> **sehr, Suppe, lesen, also** —> the **s** is pronounced [z] as in the English word *zoo*

The letter **v** is normally pronounced like an English **f** (in words of foreign origin it is often pronounced as [v])

> **Vater, von, viel, brav** —> the **v** is pronounced [f]

As in English, the letter **q** is always followed by a **u**, but in German pronounced as if it were written **kv**, as in the Yiddish word *kvetch*.

An initial **c** is pronounced as a **ts** if it comes before **e, i,** or **ä**. In other cases it is usually pronounced as [k]:

> **Cäsar, Celsius, circa** —> the **c** is pronounced [ts]

Word Stress

As a general rule the stress is on the first syllable in native German words unless the first syllable is an unstressed prefix (*See* Chap. 4). In the case of words that have been borrowed from other languages, stress patterns are much less predictable. Often they follow the rules of the language from which the word has been borrowed. There are, however, certain suffixes that have predictable stress patterns.

Suffix	German Example	Stress
-tät	**Rarität, Aktivität, Majestät**	Last syllable
-ik	**Kritik, Musik, Politik**	Last syllable
-ie	**Chemie, Poesie, Theorie**	Last syllable
-erei	**Malerei, Konditorei**	Last syllable
-eum	**Museum, Mausoleum**	Next to last syllable
-ieren	**servieren, studieren**	Next to last syllable

Chapter 2
WORD ORDER AND CONJUNCTIONS

IN THIS CHAPTER:

✔ *Word Order*
✔ *Coordinating Conjunctions*
✔ *Subordinating Conjunctions*

Word Order

The grammatical clues in German such as case, gender, and verb endings permit one to analyze the relationships between the words in a sentence without having to rely primarily on word order. Therefore, word order in German is more flexible than in English. In general, though, one begins as in English with the elements that give the most important information, the subject and the verb, followed by other parts of speech.

However, in German the verb is often composed of more than one word, where a portion of this verb complex will come at the end of the sentence. Therefore, the end of a German sentence carries as much stress as the beginning; more important items tend to move toward the end of this middle field. Some guidelines for the ordering of elements in this middle field will be provided at the appropriate places in the book (see, for example, the order of direct and indirect objects in Chap. 3, or the order of adverbial elements in Chap. 6). If the speaker wants to give a particular element greater stress, that unit of the sentence will be shifted from the basic position toward the end of the middle field. Thus, for those interested in translating, the best way to proceed in decoding a German sentence is to start at the beginning, then go to the end of the sentence and work back to the front.

Although German does exhibit substantial flexibility, there are nonetheless cardinal rules for word order that must be followed in forming sentences.

Statements

The regular word order for declarative sentences in German is:

Statements (Regular Word Order) =
Subject + Verb (+ Other Sentence Parts)

Simple Tenses

In statements in the present or simple past, the subject is in first position, the verb in second, and objects and other sentence parts follow. Words such as **danke, ja, nein, doch** do not affect word order.

Subject	*Conjugated Verb*	*Other Sentence Parts*
Der Mann	**ist**	**unser Lehrer.**
Die Erde	**dreht**	**sich um die Sonne.**
Ja, mein Bruder	**gab**	**ihm das Buch.**

Compound Tenses

In statements containing compound tenses, the conjugated verb (the verb form with the personal ending) or the auxiliary is in second position. The dependent infinitive, the double infinitive, or the past participle is in last position, preceded by the other sentence parts.

Subject	*Conjugated Verb*	*Other Sentence Parts*	*Infinitives or Past Participles*
Inge	**wird**	**ihm**	**helfen.**
Meine Eltern	**wollten**	**sich einen Ofen**	**kaufen.**

| Ich | habe | es ihr | zeigen wollen. |
| Das Auto | wurde | von ihm | gestohlen. |

Separable Prefixes

Simple Tenses

In simple tenses the prefix is separated from the verb and occurs in last position.

Subject	Conjugated Verb	Other Sentence Parts	Prefix
Wir	gehen	jeden Sonntag	spazieren.
Der Student	kam	mit dem Zug	an.

Compound Tenses

In compound tenses the prefix is attached to the verb and occurs in last or next-to-last position.

Subject	Conjugated Verb	Other Sentence Parts	Infinitives or Past Participles
Er	wird	bald	heimgehen.
Ich	habe	das Geschenk	aufgemacht.
Inge	hat	um 10 Uhr	gehen müssen.

Inverted Word Order

For special emphasis the direct object, indirect object, adverb, prepositional phrase, or any other logical unit can be placed in first position (denoted here by X). The conjugated verb remains in second position, which means that the subject comes after the verb, followed by any other sentence parts that may be present.

Inverted Word Order = X + Verb + Subject
(+ Other Sentence Parts).

If the verb is a compound verb, the conjugated form of the auxiliary verb is in second position and the past participle, dependent infinitive, or double infinitive is in final position.

It is important to remember that the X element can be of any length: a single word, a prepositional phrase, a dependent clause, or even a combination of long and involved dependent clauses. Whatever the case though, the subject and verb of the main clause must be inverted.

Any Element	Conjugated Verb	Subject	Other Sentence Parts
Gestern	**reiste**	**mein Freund**	**nach Indien.**
Im Sommer	**besuche**	**ich**	**die Großeltern.**
Wie immer	**hat**	**sie**	**ihn warten lassen.**
Wenn ich Zeit hätte	**würde**	**ich**	**sie besuchen.**

Questions

Questions introduced by an interrogative word or phrase seeking specific information, or general questions without such a word also require inverted word order. See Chap. 9 for a full explanation.

Coordinating Conjunctions

Regular Word Order

A coordinating conjunction links words, phrases, or clauses that are parallel and equal. Because coordinating conjunctions are merely links and do not become part of any of the clauses they connect, they have no effect on word order.

*Subject + Verb (+ Rest of Sentence) +
Coordinating Conjunction + Subject +
Verb (+ Other Sentence Parts)*

If, however, another element X directly follows the coordinating conjunction, the word order of the clause following the conjunction will be inverted in accordance with the rules discussed above (X + V + S).

The most common coordinating conjunctions are:

aber—*but*

> **Er mußte hier bleiben,** *aber* **ich durfte ins Kino gehen.**
> *He had to stay here, but I was allowed to go to the movies.*

denn—*because, since, for*
> **Sie geht nicht mit,** *denn* **sie ist krank.**
> *She isn't going along, because she is ill.*

oder—*or*
> **Sag ihm die Wahrheit,** *oder* **er wird sie von mir hören.**
> *Tell him the truth, or he'll hear it from me.*

sondern—*but (on the contrary / rather)* **Sondern** follows a negative.
> **Sie fuhr nicht in die Stadt,** *sondern* **sie blieb zu Hause.**
> *She didn't drive into town, but (rather) she stayed home.*

und—*and*
> **Ich habe im Gras gelegen,** *und* **er hat gearbeitet.**
> *I was lying in the grass, and he was working.*

Subordinating Conjunctions

Verb in Final Position

Subordinating conjunctions introduce dependent clauses (sometimes also referred to as subordinate clauses). Dependent clauses cannot stand alone and establish the relationship between the main clause and the dependent clause or clauses in the sentence. Thus, they have an effect on word order: the conjugated verb is normally placed in final position at the end of the dependent clause.

Subordinating Conjunction + Subject
(+ Other Sentence Parts) + Verb)

All dependent clauses introduced by subordinating conjunctions are separated from the main clause by a comma. The most common subordinating conjunctions include:

als ob—*as if*
> **Sie sieht aus,** *als ob* **sie krank gewesen wäre.**
> *She looks as if she had been ill.*

bevor—before
Bevor du ins Kino gehst, mußt du mir noch helfen.
Before you go to the movies, you have to help me.

bis—*until*
Ich arbeitete, *bis* ich müde wurde.
I worked until I became tired.

da—*since, as*
Ich mußte warten, *da* sie noch nicht angezogen war.
I had to wait since she wasn't dressed yet.

damit—*in order to, so that*
Ich rufe ihn an, *damit* er nicht kommt.
I'll call him so that he won't come.

daß—*that*
Ich weiß, *daß* er einen Hund hat.
I know that he has a dog.

nachdem—*after*
Er grüßte mich, *nachdem* ich ihn gegrüßt hatte.
He greeted me after I had greeted him.

ob—*whether, if*
Sie wollen wissen, *ob* sie rauchen dürfen.
They want to know whether they may smoke.

obwohl—*although*
Er ging, *obwohl* es sein Vater verboten hatte.
He went although his father had forbidden it.

seit, seitdem—*since*
Seitdem wir weniger Geld haben, bleiben wir öfters zu Hause.
Since we have less money, we stay home more often.

während—*while*
Ich arbeitete, *während* er einen Roman las.
I worked while he read a novel.

weil—*because*

> **Wir konnten nichts kaufen,** *weil* **wir kein Geld hatten.**
> *We couldn't buy anything because we had no money.*

als, wenn, wann

The English *when* can be expressed three ways in German: **als, wenn, wann.** Each has a definite use, and is not interchangeable.

Als refers to a single action in the past. It is used with the simple past, the present perfect, or the past perfect tense.

> **Ich freute mich,** *als* **er die Goldmedaille gewann.**
> *I was glad when he won the gold medal.*

Wenn corresponds to English *if* in conditional clauses. In time clauses it may be rendered with *when.* It is then used with the present tense, referring to the future.

> *Wenn* **ich Zeit hätte,** *würde* **ich schwimmen gehen.**
> *If had time, I would go swimming.*

> **Ich gehe schwimmen,** *wenn* **es heiß wird.**
> *I'll go swimming when it gets hot.*

Wenn may also be used with the simple past tense. It then has the meaning of *whenever.*

> *Wenn* **er hier** *war,* **gingen wir spazieren.**
> *Whenever he was here, we went for a walk.*

Wann is an interrogative used in direct and indirect questions.

> *Wann* **erwartest du ihn?**   *When do you expect him?*
> **Weißt du,** *wann* **Ilse kommt?** *Do you know when Ilse is*
>   *coming?*

Chapter 3
NOUNS AND ARTICLES

IN THIS CHAPTER:

✔ *Gender*
✔ *Cases of Nouns*
✔ *Special Uses of the Definite and Indefinite Articles*
✔ *Omission of the Indefinite or Definite Article*

Gender

der, die, das

Unlike English all German nouns have a grammatical gender. A noun can be masculine, feminine, or neuter regardless of its natural gender.

The definite article **der** *(the)* designates a masculine noun, **die** *(the)* designates a feminine noun, and **das** *(the)* a neuter noun.

Nouns that refer specifically to male beings, such as *father* or *uncle*, are usually masculine. Those that refer to female beings, such as *mother* or *daughter*, are usually feminine. However, nouns referring to things are not necessarily neuter. For this reason the gender of each noun must be memorized.

Although no definite rules for gender can be given, the following generalizations may be helpful in memorizing the gender of frequently used nouns.

13

Gender Identification by Noun Groups

Nouns Referring to People:

Nouns referring to male beings (people and animals) are usually masculine. Nouns referring to female beings are usually feminine.

Masculine:		*Feminine:*	
der Vater	*father*	**die Mutter**	*mother*
der Mann	*man*	**die Frau**	*Mrs., woman*
der Sohn	*son*	**die Tochter**	*daughter*
der Bruder	*brother*	**die Schwester**	*sister*
der Herr	*Mr., gentleman*	**die Dame**	*lady*
der Sänger	*singer (male)*	**die Sängerin**	*singer (fem.)*
der Lehrer	*teacher (male)*	**die Lehrerin**	*teacher (fem.)*
der Hahn	*rooster*	**die Henne**	*chicken*

Nouns referring to young people and young animals are usually neuter.

Neuter:			
das Mädchen	*girl*	**das Kind**	*child*
das Fräulein	*Miss, young woman*	**das Kalb**	*calf*
das Kätzchen	*kitten*	**das Küken**	*chick*
das Schwesterlein	*little sister*	**das Fohlen**	*foal*
das Tischlein	*little table*	**das Lamm**	*lamb*

Note!

All diminutives ending in **-chen** or **-lein** are neuter, regardless of the gender of the stem noun.

Masculine Nouns:

Names of all days of the week, all the calendar months, and all seasons are masculine. See Chapter 7 for a complete list.

Names of all cardinal directions

der Süden	*south*	**der Westen**	*west*
der Norden	*north*	**der Osten**	*east*

Feminine Nouns:

Names of most trees

die Tanne	*fir*
die Linde	*linden tree*
But: **der Ahorn**	*maple*

Names of most fruits

die Banane	*banana*
die Pflaume	*plum*
But: **der Apfel**	*apple*

Names of most flowers

die Orchidee	*orchid*
die Lilie	*lily*

Neuter Nouns:

Names of cities

das historische München	*historical Munich*
das große Hongkong	*large Hong Kong*

Names of most countries

das neutrale Schweden	*neutral Sweden*
das moderne Deutschland	*modern Germany*

The neuter article for cities and countries is used only if the noun is modified. Without a modifier one simply uses **München, Berlin, Schweden, Deutschland, Italien,** etc.

Exceptions:

Note, however, that the names of the following countries are not neuter but feminine:

die Schweiz	*Switzerland*
die Türkei	*Turkey*
die Tschechische Republik	*Czech Republic*

Still others are masculine:

der Iran	*Iran*
der Iraq	*Iraq*

The following are used only in the plural:

die Niederlande	*Netherlands*
die Vereinigten Staaten	*United States*
die USA	*USA*

The above exceptions are always used with their articles, whether or not they are modified.

Wir besuchen die Schweiz.

Names of metals and chemical elements

das Gold	*gold*	**das Helium**	*helium*
das Kupfer	*copper*	*But:* **der Stahl**	*steel*

Essential Point

All German nouns and words used as nouns are capitalized, regardless of their position in the sentence: **der Herr, das Haus, die Alte, der Junge, das Auto, die Frau, das Lesen, das Singen.**

Cases of Nouns

German has four cases which signal how nouns and pronouns are used within a sentence, clause, or phrase. The cases are:

> **nominative**
> **accusative**
> **dative**
> **genitive**

The grammatical functions reflected by these four cases correspond more or less to the subject, direct object, indirect object, and possessive cases in English usage. The articles and/or adjectives preceding a noun change their forms to indicate the case of that noun. As in English, there are two types of article in German, the *definite article* and the *indefinite article.*

The *definite article* (**der, das, die**) is used to refer to a *particular* or *specific* person, place, or thing.

Der **Arzt ist heute nicht hier.**   *The doctor is not here today.*

(Here we are speaking of a particular doctor.)

The *indefinite article* (**ein, ein, eine**) is used to refer to an *unspecified* person, place, or thing.

Ein **Arzt hat viele Patienten.**   *A doctor has many patients.*

As noted at the beginning of this chapter, it is the definite article that most clearly indicates the *gender* of a noun. Due to the changes in the endings of the definite article, it is also most useful in identifying the *case* of a noun. The group of words that take the same grammatical endings as the definite article are referred to as **"der"** words.

dieser	*this*	**mancher**	*many (a)*
jeder	*each, every*	**solcher**	*such*
jener	*that*	**welcher**	*which*

Similarly, the group of words that take the same grammatical endings as the indefinite article are referred to as **"ein"** words.

mein	*my*	**ihr**	*her or their*
dein	*your* (familiar, sing.)	**unser**	*our*
sein	*his or its*	**euer**	*your* (familiar, pl.)
		Ihr	*your* (formal)

These **"ein"** words are also referred to as *possessive adjectives,* since their function is to describe the nouns they modify by indicating possession or ownership.

Note that **kein,** *no, not any* is also an **"ein"** word.

Nominative Case

The nominative forms of the definite and indefinite articles and of the **"der"** and **"ein"** words are as follows.

	Singular			*Plural*
	Masculine	*Neuter*	*Feminine*	*All genders*
Definite article				
"der" words	**der**	**das**	**die**	**die**
	dieser	**dieses**	**diese**	**diese**
	jener	**jenes**	**jene**	**jene**
	welcher	**welches**	**welche**	**welche**
Indefinite article				
"ein" words	**ein**	**ein**	**eine**	(no plural)
	mein	**mein**	**meine**	**meine**
	ihr	**ihr**	**ihre**	**ihre**
	unser	**unser**	**unsere**	**unsere**
Negative article	**kein**	**kein**	**keine**	**keine**

Remember!

Ihr your (formal) takes the same endings as **ihr** (her or their).

The nominative case is used in German in several ways:

As the Subject of the Verb

Der Mann **spielt Golf.**	*The man is playing golf.*
Die Freundin **kommt.**	*The girlfriend is coming.*
Ein Hund **bellt.**	*A dog is barking.*
Meine Eltern **wohnen dort.**	*My parents live there.*

As a Predicate Nominative

A predicate nominative is a noun (or pronoun) that follows a linking verb and refers back to and is equated with the subject of the sentence or clause. Common linking verbs include:

sein *(to be)*	**werden** *(to become)*	**bleiben** *(to remain)*
heissen *(to be called, named)*		**scheinen** *(to appear)*

Martin ist *unser Freund.*	*Martin is our friend.*
Gisela wird *keine Ärztin.*	*Gisela will not become a doctor.*
Der Hund heißt *Waldi.*	*The dog is named Waldi.*

The Accusative Case

The accusative forms of the definite and indefinite articles and of the **"der"** and **"ein"** words are as follows.

| | Singular | | | Plural |
	Masculine	Neuter	Feminine	All genders
Definite article				
"der" words	**den**	**das**	**die**	**die**
	diesen	**dieses**	**diese**	**diese**
	welchen	**welches**	**welche**	**welche**
Indefinite article				
"ein" words	**einen**	**ein**	**eine**	(no plural)
	meinen	**mein**	**meine**	**meine**
	ihren	**ihr**	**ihre**	**ihre**
Negative article	**keinen**	**kein**	**keine**	**keine**

The accusative case is used in several ways:

As the Direct Object of the Verb

Wir kaufen *den Wagen.*	*We are buying the car.*
Ich nehme *die Zeitung.*	*I take the newspaper.*
Welchen Mann *kennst du?*	*Which man do you know?*
Ich habe *kein Geld.*	*I have no money.*

With Expressions of Definite Time and Duration of Time

Er bleibt *eine Woche* **in Bonn.**	*He is staying in Bonn one week.*
Sie besucht mich *jeden Tag.*	*She visits me every day.*

With Prepositions

The accusative case is used as the object of certain prepositions, which are discussed in Chapter 8.

Dative Case

The dative forms of the definite and indefinite articles and of the **"der"** and **"ein"** words are as follows.

	Singular			*Plural*
	Masculine	Neuter	Feminine	All genders
Definite article				
"der" words	**dem**	**dem**	**der**	**den**
	diesem	**diesem**	**dieser**	**diesen**
	jenem	**jenem**	**jener**	**jenen**
Indefinite article				
"ein" words	**einem**	**einem**	**einer**	(no plural)
	meinem	**meinem**	**meiner**	**meinen**
	ihrem	**ihrem**	**ihrer**	**ihren**
Negative article	**keinem**	**keinem**	**keiner**	**keinen**

Remember!

The dative plural noun always adds **-n,** unless the nominative plural form already ends in **-n** or **-s.**

Ich schicke *den Kindern* **Bilder.**	*I send pictures to the children.*
Wir geben *den Männern* **nichts.**	*We give nothing to the men.*
Marta schickt *ihren Eltern* **Bilder.**	*Marta sends pictures to her parents.*

The dative case is used in several ways:

As the Indirect Object of the Verb

In English this relationship is often expressed by the prepositions *to* or *for.* The person or animal to whom something is given, shown, or told is in the dative case.

Ich gebe *dem Mann* **das Geld.**   *I am giving money to the man.*
Er kauft *der Frau* **die Bluse.**   *He buys a blouse for the woman.*
Ich sage *meiner Freundin* **nichts.**   *I say nothing to my girlfriend.*
Er kauft *seinem Kind* **Schokolade.**   *He buys chocolate for his child*

In sentences with only one object, it tends to be the direct object. However, there are many verbs in German that are used with both a direct and an indirect object. In these cases, the direct object is usually a thing and the indirect object in the dative is usually a person.

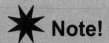 **Note!**

If the direct object is in the form of a noun, it follows the indirect object. If it is in the form of a pronoun, it precedes the indirect object.

bringen	*to bring, take*	**Er bringt** *seiner Freundin* **Blumen.** *He brings flowers to his girlfriend.*
geben	*to give*	**Wir geben** *der Katze* **Milch.** *We are giving milk to the cat.* **Wir geben** *sie* **der Katze.** *(The direct object is a pronoun here.)*
kaufen	*to buy*	**Sie kauft** *ihrer Mutter* **einen Wagen.** *She is buying a car for her mother.*
schicken	*to send*	**Sonja schickt** *ihrer Tante* **ein Buch.** *Sonja is sending her aunt a book.* **Sonja schickt** *es* **ihr.** *(The direct object is a pronoun here.)*
sagen	*to say, tell*	**Sie sagt** *ihrem Mann* **die Wahrheit.** *She tells her husband the truth.*

With Dative Verbs

A number of German verbs take only dative objects. The following commonly used verbs are always used with the dative case.

antworten	*to answer*	**Ich antworte** *dem Herrn.*
		I answer the gentleman.
danken	*to thank (for)*	**Wir danken** *unserem Lehrer.*
		We thank our teacher.
helfen	*to help*	**Ich helfe** *dem Kind.*
		I am helping the child.
gehören	*to belong*	**Dieses Buch gehört** *ihrem Sohn.*
		This book belongs to her son.
gefallen	*to like,*	**Jener Hut gefällt** *seiner Frau*
	be pleasing	*His wife likes that hat.*
folgen	*to follow*	**Der Hund folgt** *mir* **nach Hause.**
		The dog follows me home.

The verb **glauben** is used with the dative when followed by a person. The accusative is used when it is followed by a thing.

Ich glaube *dem Kind.*	*I believe the child.*
Ich glaube *die Geschichte.*	*I believe the story.*

Don't Forget!

Many impersonal constructions also require the dative case.

Es geht *mir* **gut.**	*I'm fine (doing well).*
Es tut *mir* **leid.**	*I'm sorry.*
Es schmeckt *mir.*	*It tastes good (to me).*

With Prepositions

The dative case is used with certain prepositions, which are presented in Chapter 8.

Genitive Case

The genitive forms of the definite and indefinite articles and of the "**der**" and "**ein**" words are as follows.

| | *Singular* | | | *Plural* |
	Masculine	*Neuter*	*Feminine*	*All genders*
Definite article				
"**der**" words	**des**	**des**	**der**	**der**
	dieses	**dieses**	**dieser**	**dieser**
	jenes	**jenes**	**jener**	**jener**
Indefinite article				
"**ein**" words	**eines**	**eines**	**einer**	(no plural)
	meines	**meines**	**meiner**	**meiner**
	ihres	**ihres**	**ihrer**	**ihrer**
Negative article	**keines**	**keines**	**keiner**	**keiner**

The genitive case is used in several ways:

To Show Possession or Relationship Between Two Nouns

In English this is expressed by the preposition *of* or with '*s*. The apostrophe is not normally used in German. (See exception below.)

Dort liegt das Buch *des Lehrers.*	*There lies the teacher's book.*
Wo ist das Auto *der Frau?*	*Where is the woman's car?*
Das ist die Frau *meines Sohnes.*	*That is my son's wife.*
Hier ist ein Foto *unseres Hauses.*	*Here is a picture of our house.*

Das ist das Haus *meiner Eltern.*	*That is my parents' house.*
Frau Hämels **Mann ist hier.**	*Mrs. Hämel's husband is here.*

In German the genitive noun generally follows the noun that it modifies, whereas in English the possessive noun usually precedes the noun it modifies.

der Wagen *meines Onkels*	*my uncle's car*
das Buch *des Mädchens*	*the girl's book*
die Bluse *unserer Tante*	*our aunt's blouse*

However, when a proper name is put into the genitive in German, it usually precedes the noun it modifies.

Uwes **Wagen**	*Uwe's car*
Mariannes **Buch**	*Marianne's book*

With Expressions of Indefinite Time

In English these are expressed with *one day, some day (night, etc.).*

Eines Tages **wird er kommen.**	*Some day he'll come.*
Eines Morgens **besuchte er uns.**	*One morning he visited us.*

By way of analogy the feminine noun **Nacht** also adds **-s** in such time expressions.

Eines Nachts **war er wieder gesund.** *One night he was well again.*

Note!

A very small number of verbs take a genitive object. These constructions often sound rather formal and somewhat archaic.

Wir gedenken *unserer Gefallenen.*
   We remember our fallen.
Er rühmt sich *seines Talentes.*
   He brags about his talents.

With Prepositions

The genitive case is used with certain prepositions, which are presented in Chapter 3.

Noun Endings in the Genitive Case

-s or -es endings

Most masculine and neuter nouns add **-s** or **-es** in the singular. No apostrophe is used. An **-s** is added if the masculine or neuter noun has more than one syllable, such as **meines Bruder***s***, dieses Zimmer***s***.

An **-es** is added if the masculine or neuter noun has only one syllable, such as **des Buch***es***. If the last syllable is accented, the genitive ending is also **-es,** such as **des Gedicht***es***.

There are no special endings for the genitive plural noun form.

-ns or -ens endings

Some nouns add **-ens** to form the genitive singular, such as **des Herz***ens***, des Nam***ens***, des Fried***ens***

Feminine

No ending is added to feminine nouns in the genitive case.

Wo ist das Auto *der Frau?*   *Where is the woman's car?*

Proper names

An **-s** is added to proper names in the genitive case.

Luises **Bruder spielt Fussball.**   *Louise's brother plays soccer.*
Frau Bauers **Hut war teuer.**   *Mrs. Bauer's hat was expensive.*

When a masculine name ends in a sibilant (an *s* sound), the genitive can be formed by adding **-ens** or an apostrophe.

Maxens Geburtstag **ist am 5. Mai.**   *Max's birthday is May 5th.*
Max' Geburtstag **ist am 5. Mai.**   *Max's birthday is May 5th.*

However, the **von** construction is preferred in such cases.

Der Geburtstag *von Max* **ist am 5. Mai.**

Substitute for the Genitive Case

Note: In informal speech a dative construction is often substituted for the more formal sounding genitive.

Das Kleid *meiner Tochter* **war teuer.**
My daughter's dress was expensive.
Das Kleid *von meiner Tochter* **war teuer.**

Der Wagen *meines Bruders* **ist kaputt.**
My brother's car is broken.
Der Wagen *von meinem Bruder* **ist kaputt.**

Noun Endings in the Accusative, Dative, and Genitive Cases

There is a small group of masculine nouns that add an **-n** or **-en** ending to the noun in the accusative, dative, and genitive singular. These nouns are often referred to as *weak nouns* or *n-nouns*.

Although many of these nouns must simply be memorized, it is helpful to remember that masculine nouns formed from adjectives and verb participles **(der Junge, der Alte, der Reisende)** fall into this category as well as masculine nouns ending in **-ent** and **-ist (der Student, der Tourist).**

Examples of other masculine nouns that belong to this group:

der Held	*hero*	**der Mensch**	*human being*
der Herr	*gentleman*	**der Junge**	*boy*

Wir treffen *den Studenten.* *We meet the student.*
Ich gebe *dem Herrn* **die Krawatte.** *I give the tie to the gentleman.*
Die Frau *des Präsidenten* **ist krank.** *The president's wife is ill.*

Special Uses of the Definite Article

With General or Abstract Nouns:

Die Katze **ist ein Haustier.** *A (the) cat is a domestic animal.*
Die Liebe **ist eine Himmelsmacht.** *Love is a heavenly power.*
Das Leben **ist kurz.** *Life is short.*

With Names of Streets, Lakes, Mountains, and Countries:

Die Hofstraße **ist in München.**	*Hof Street is in Munich.*
Der Bodensee **ist tief.**	*Lake Constance is deep.*
Der Tafelberg **ist in Afrika.**	*Table Mountain is in Africa.*

The definite article is not used with countries that are neuter, unless the name of the country is modified.

Deutschland **produziert viel.**	*Germany produces much.*
Das moderne Deutschland **produziert viel.**	

With Weights, Measures, and Expressions of Time:

The accusative case of the definite article is used in German with expressions of weight, measure, and time. In English the indefinite article is used in the sense of *per.*

Das kostet 2 Mark *das Pfund.*	*That costs 2 marks a pound.*
Es kostet 50 Pfennig *das Meter.*	*It costs 50 pfennig a meter.*
Er kommt einmal *die Woche.*	*He comes once a week.*
Wir bezahlen zweimal *den Monat.*	*We pay twice a month.*

You Need to Know ✔

The definite article is used in German to refer to parts of the body or articles of clothing, unless there is doubt as to the identity of the possessor. In English the possessive is used.

Er zieht sich *den Mantel* **an.**	*He is putting on his coat.*
Ich wasche mir *das Gesicht.*	*I am washing my face.*

Omission of the Indefinite or Definite Article

The indefinite or definite article is omitted in the following cases:

Before a Predicate Nominative

> **Sie ist** *Russin.* — *She is a Russian.*
> **Er wird** *Zahnarzt.* — *He will become a dentist.*

If the predicate nominative is modified, the article is expressed.

> **Er ist** *ein bekannter Pianist.* — *He is a well-known pianist.*
> **Er ist** *der beste Lehrer.* — *He is the best teacher.*

With Certain Set Phrases

> **Sie hat** *Fieber.* — *She has a fever.*
> **Wir haben** *Kopfweh.* — *We have a headache.*
> **Hast du** *Zahnweh?* — *Do you have a toothache?*

After the Conjunction **als,** *meaning* "*as a(n)*"

> **Er arbeitet dort als** *Ingenieur.* — *He works there as an engineer.*
> **Sie ist als** *Studentin* **in Berlin.** — *She is in Berlin as a student.*

Chapter 4
VERBS

IN THIS CHAPTER:

✔ Verb Overview
✔ Verb Tenses
✔ Reflexive Verbs
✔ Modal Auxiliary Verbs
✔ The Imperative
✔ The Conditional and
   the Subjunctive
✔ The Passive Voice

Verb Overview

In German, as in English, verbs are words that express an action, a process, or a state of being; for example, to *read, to get, to become.*

Transitive and Intransitive Verbs

Also, as in English, in German verbs are divided into two basic grammatical categories—*transitive verbs* and *intransitive verbs*. A transitive verb is a verb that can take a direct object. Take, for example, the verb *to describe. He describes* can be expanded to show *what* he describes. An intransitive verb is one that *cannot* take a direct object. Examples of intransitive verbs are *to live, to travel, to die.* Some verbs may be used either as transitive verbs or as intransitive verbs, e.g., *he whistled as he worked* and *he whistled a tune.*

Personal Endings

German, like English, distinguishes between the *first person,* the *second person,* and the *third person.* Moreover, each person can be either singular or plural. The present and past tense personal endings that indicate these persons are introduced later in this chapter.

Certain forms of the verb, such as the infinitive, the present participle, and the past participle, do not take personal endings. In a phrase, only one part of the verb is conjugated (i.e. takes an ending).

Verb Tenses

In German, as in other languages, verbs have *tense;* that is, different forms of the verb indicate the time when the action of the verb takes place, e.g. present, past, or future tense

Strong Verbs and Weak Verbs

There are two basic types of verbs in German: *strong verbs* and *weak verbs.* Weak verbs keep the same stem vowel throughout all their forms, and strong verbs have stem vowel changes in their past tenses. As a *general* rule, the weak verbs have regular and predictable forms, whereas the strong verbs are irregular. Since, however, there are irregular weak verbs and certain predictable patterns for the strong verbs, we will not

Don't Forget

Since the patterns for the strong verbs and the irregular weak verbs are not fully predictable, it is essential to learn **all** the principal parts of such verbs when they are first introduced.

use the terms regular and irregular verbs, but will instead refer to verbs as *weak, strong,* or *mixed.*

The three principal parts of a verb that must be learned are the *infinitive,* the *past tense,* and the *past participle.* In some cases a fourth form of the German verb must also be memorized—the second or third person singular of the present tense, since a small group of strong verbs also have vowel changes in these forms. (The most common strong and mixed German verbs are summarized in the Appendix.)

Speakers of English are already familiar with the phenomenon that some verbs have no vowel changes in their various forms while others do. Compare, for example, regular verbs such as *play, played, played* or *paint, painted, painted* with irregular verbs such as *sing, sang, sung* or *think, thought, thought.*

Study the principal parts of strong and weak verbs as illustrated by the verbs **spielen** (to *play)* and **singen** *(to sing).*

Weak Verb		*Strong Verb*	
Infinitive	**spielen**	Infinitive	**singen**
Past tense	**spielte**	Past tense	**sang**
Past participle	**gespielt**	Past participle	**gesungen**

Simple Present Tense

Weak and Strong Verbs

The simple present tense of both the weak and the strong verbs is formed by adding the personal endings for the present tense to the infinitive stem.

Simple Present = Infinitive Stem + Present Tense Personal Ending

In German the infinitive is the dictionary form of the verb. Typically the infinitive ends in **-n** or **-en**. The *infinitive stem* is derived by dropping the **-en** or **-n** from the infinitive.

Infinitive	*Infinitive Stem*
denken	**denk-**
singen	**sing-**
handeln	**handel-**

wandern	wander-
tun	tu-

The present tense personal endings that must be added to the infinitive stem are:

	Singular	Plural
First person	-e	-en
Second person	-st	-t
Third person	-t	-en

Thus, the fully conjugated present tense of **denken** is:

ich denke	**wir denken**
du denkst	**ihr denkt**
er	
sie denkt	**sie denken**
es	
	Sie denken

Note!

Since the same personal ending is used for **er, sie,** and **es,** all conjugations presented in this book for third person singular will list only **er. Sie** (the form for "you" formal) takes the same personal ending as **sie** (they) and thus will not be listed separately in the conjugations below.

There is only one present tense in German. Thus, the three forms of the present tense in English, *I think, I do think,* and *I am thinking,* are all translated with **ich denke.** Here are some examples.

Wir *kaufen* **einen Wagen.**	*We are buying a car.*
Ich *kenne* **den Mann.**	*I know the man.*
Sie *studieren* **Englisch.**	*They study English.*

Variations in Personal Endings

Additional **e**

When the infinitive stem ends in **-d, -t, -m, -n,** preceded by a consonant other than **-l, -r,** the endings in the second and third person singular and second person plural are expanded by adding an **-e** before the personal endings. Thus, the fully conjugated form for **arbeiten** is:

ich arbeite	wir arbeiten
du arbeit*e*st	ihr arbeit*e*t
er arbeit*e*t	sie arbeiten

Sie *badet* **das Kind.**	*She is bathing the child.*
Er *atmet* **langsam.**	*He is breathing slowly.*
Warum *öffnest* **du die Tür?**	*Why do you open the door?*

No additional **s** *sound*

When the stem of the infinitive ends in **-s, -ß, -x, -z,** the personal ending for the second person singular is just **-t.**

Warum *haßt* **du ihn?**	*Why do you hate him?*
Tanzt **du gern?**	*Do you like to dance?*

Stem Vowel Changes in Strong Verbs in the Present Tense

Many German strong verbs have a vowel change in the stem of the present tense in the second and third person singular. There is no vowel change in the other persons. Most strong verbs containing **a, au, e** undergo this vowel change. They can be grouped according to the changes that take place.

Changes from **a, au** *to* **ä, äu**

ich fahre	ich falle	ich trage	ich laufe
du fährst	du fällst	du trägst	du läufst
er fährt	er fällt	er trägt	er läuft

Changes from **e** *to* **i, ie**

Most strong verbs with an **e** in the infinite stem change their stem vowels to **i** or **ie** in the second and third person singular.

ich esse	**ich breche**	**ich lese**	**ich sehe**
du ißt	**du brichst**	**du liest**	**du siehst**
er ißt	**er bricht**	**er liest**	**er sieht**

Irregular Verbs

The present tense forms of **sein** (*to be*), **haben** (*to have*), **werden** (*to get, become*), **wissen** (*to know*), and **tun** (*to do*) are irregular.

sein	*haben*	*werden*	*wissen*	*tun*
ich bin	**ich habe**	**ich werde**	**ich weiß**	**ich tue**
du bist	**du hast**	**du wirst**	**du weißt**	**du tust**
er ist	**er hat**	**er wird**	**er weiß**	**er tut**
wir sind	**wir haben**	**wir werden**	**wir wissen**	**wir tun**
ihr seid	**ihr habt**	**ihr werdet**	**ihr wißt**	**ihr tut**
sie sind	**sie haben**	**sie werden**	**sie wissen**	**sie tun**

Special Uses of the Present Tense

The present tense in German can be used to indicate that an event will take place in the future. The future meaning is conveyed by the context or by an adverbial expression indicating future time.

Ich *gehe* **morgen nach Hause.**	*I'm going home tomorrow.*
Fährst **du nächste Woche**	*Are you driving to Frankfurt*
nach Frankfurt?	*next week?*

The present tense is also used to express the fact that an action started in the past continues into the present. The time element is usually introduced by **schon** or **seit**, corresponding to English *for.*

Er *wohnt schon* **zwei Jahre hier**	*He's been living here for two years.*
Er *ist seit* **einer Woche in Paris.**	*He has been in Paris for one week.*

Simple Past Tense

In German the simple past tense (also referred to as the imperfect or preterite) describes a completed action or a chain of events that took place in the past. This tense is generally not used in conversation, but is the customary tense used in written narratives. For this reason it is sometimes referred to as the *narrative* past.

Weak Verbs

The simple past tense of the weak verbs is formed by adding the past tense marker **-t** plus the personal endings for weak verbs to the infinitive stems. The German past tense marker **–t** corresponds to the English past tense marker **–d**, e.g. **sagte, machte, spielte**; *said, made, played.* Note that there are no changes in the stem vowels in the simple past tense of weak verbs.

> *Infinitive Stem + Past Tense Marker* **-t** *+ Weak Personal Ending*

The full pattern for all persons is as follows:

	Singular	*Plural*
First person	**-te**	**-ten**
Second person	**-test**	**-tet**
Third person	**-te**	**-ten**

Study the past tense forms in the following sentences:

Wir *tanzten* **den ganzen Abend.**	*We danced the whole evening.*
Ich *machte* **damals eine Reise.**	*I took a trip at that time.*

Spieltest du als Kind Klavier?   *Did you play piano as a child?*
Sie *fragte* den Lehrer.   *She asked the teacher.*

When the infinitive stem ends in **-d, -t**, or in **-m, -n** preceded by a consonant other than **-l, -r**, an **-e-** is inserted before the above endings to ensure that the tense marker will be heard clearly. Study the verb forms below:

ich arbeitete	**ich tötete**	**ich badete**	**ich öffnete**
du arbeitetest	**du tötetest**	**du badetest**	**du öffnetest**
er arbeitete	**er tötete**	**er badete**	**er öffnete**

Irregular Weak Verbs

The following weak verbs are irregular in that in addition to the past tense marker **-t** they have stem vowel changes in the simple past:

Infinitive	*Simple Past*	*Infinitive*	*Simple Past*
brennen	**brannte**	**senden**	**sandte**
kennen	**kannte**	**bringen**	**brachte**
nennen	**nannte**	**denken**	**dachte**
rennen	**rannte**	**wissen**	**wußte**

Strong Verbs

In strong verbs a stem vowel change rather than the tense marker **-t** marks the past tense. The simple past of strong verbs is formed by adding the past tense personal endings to the past tense stem.

Past Tense Stem + Strong Past Tense Personal Ending

The past tense personal endings of strong verbs is as follows:

	Singular	*Plural*
First person	—	**-en**
Second person	**-st**	**-t**
Third person	—	**-en**

Note that the first and third person singular take **no** personal endings in the simple past tense.

The full conjugation of the simple past tense of the strong verb **bleiben** is as follows:

ich blieb	**wir blieben**
du bliebst	**ihr bliebt**
er blieb	**sie blieben**

Vowel Changes in Stem

To help remember the different patterns of vowel changes found in the past tense stems of strong verbs, the following groupings can help.

Changes from **a, au, ei,e** *to* **ie, i**

Infinitive		*Simple Past*	*Past Participle*
a		*ie*	
fallen	*to fall*	**fiel**	*gefallen*
halten	*to stop, hold*	**hielt**	*gehalten*
lassen	*to let*	**ließ**	*gelassen*
schlafen	*to sleep*	**schlief**	*geschlafen*
au		*ie*	
laufen	*to run*	**lief**	*gelaufen*
ei		*ie*	
bleiben	*to stay*	**blieb**	*geblieben*
leihen	*to loan*	**lieh**	*geliehen*
schreiben	*to write*	**schrieb**	*geschrieben*
steigen	*to climb*	**stieg**	*gestiegen*
ei		*i*	
beißen	*to bite*	**biß**	*gebissen*
leiden	*to suffer*	**litt**	*gelitten*
reiten	*to ride*	**ritt**	*geritten*

	e			*ü*	
gehen		*to go, walk*	**ging**		*gegangen*

	a			*i*	
fangen		*to catch*	**fing**		*gefangen*

Changes from **e, ie, au** *to* **o**

Infinitive			Simple Past		Past Participle
	ie			*o*	
fliegen		*to fly*	**flog**		*geflogen*
fliehen		*to flee*	**floh**		*geflohen*
fließen		*to flow*	**floß**		*geflossen*
riechen		*to smell*	**roch**		*gerochen*
schießen		*to shoot*	**schoß**		*geschossen*
verlieren		*to lose*	**verlor**		*verloren*
ziehen		*to pull*	**zog**		*gezogen*

	au			*o*	
saufen		*to drink (of animals)*	**soff**		*gesoffen*

	e			*o*	
heben		*to lift*	**hob**		*gehoben*

Changes from **e, i, ie, o u** *to* **a**

Infinitive			Simple Past		Past Participle
	e			*a*	
brechen		*to break*	**brach**		*gebrochen*
essen		*to eat*	**aß**		*gegessen*
geben		*to give*	**gab**		*gegeben*
helfen		*to help*	**half**		*geholfen*
lesen		*to read*	**las**		*gelesen*
nehmen		*to take*	**nahm**		*genommen*
sehen		*to see*	**sah**		*gesehen*
sprechen		*to speak*	**sprach**		*gesprochen*
stehen		*to stand*	**stand**		*gestanden*
sterben		*to die*	**starb**		*gestorben*
treffen		*to meet*	**traf**		*getroffen*

vergessen	*to forget*	**vergaß**	*vergessen*
werfen	*to throw*	**warf**	*geworfen*

i			*a*
beginnen	*to begin*	**begann**	*begonnen*
bitten	*to ask*	**bat**	*gebeten*
finden	*to find*	**fand**	*gefunden*
gewinnen	*to win*	**gewann**	*gewonnen*
schwimmen	*to swim*	**schwamm**	*geschwommen*
singen	*to sing*	**sang**	*gesungen*
sitzen	*to sit*	**saß**	*gesessen*
springen	*to jump*	**sprang**	*gesprungen*
trinken	*to drink*	**trank**	*getrunken*

ie			*a*
liegen	*to lie*	**lag**	*gelegen*

o			*a*
kommen	*to come*	**kam**	*gekommen*

u			*a*
tun	*to do*	**tat**	*getan*

Changes from **a** *to* **u**

Infinitive		*Simple Past*	*Past Participle*
a		*u*	
fahren	*to drive, go*	**fuhr**	*gefahren*
schlagen	*to hit*	**schlug**	*geschlagen*
tragen	*to carry, wear*	**trug**	*getragen*
waschen	*to wash*	**wusch**	*gewaschen*

Auxiliary Verbs sein, haben, werden

The simple past tense of these auxiliary verbs is not restricted to narration as is the case with other verbs. All simple past forms of these verbs are freely used in conversation. Study the following:

ich war	**ich hatte**	**ich wurde**	
du warst	**du hattest**	**du wurdest**	
er war	**er hatte**	**er wurde**	
wir waren	**wir hatten**	**wir wurden**	
ihr wart	**ihr hattet**	**ihr wurdet**	
sie waren	**sie hatten**	**sie wurden**	

Present Perfect Tense

The present perfect tense of German verbs consists of the present tense inflected forms of the auxiliary **haben** or **sein** plus the past participle of the main verb.

Verbs that take **haben** as their auxiliary include the transitive verbs (they take a direct object), reflexive verbs, and the modal auxiliaries. Intransitive verbs (those without a direct object) indicating a change of condition or a change in location take **sein** as their auxiliary.

The German present perfect tense can refer to completed actions in the past as well as to actions that have begun in the past and continue into the present. The present perfect tense, also called the conversational past, is the past tense that **is most frequently used for past events in normal conversation**. In this situation it is best translated by the simple past tense in English.

> *Present Perfect = Present Tense of* **sein** *or* **haben** *+ Past Participle*

Formation of the Past Participle

Past Participle of weak verbs

The past participle of most weak verbs is formed by placing the prefix **ge-** in front of the infinitive stem and adding **-t** or -**et** at the end of the stem.

> *Past Participle (Weak Verbs) =* **ge-** *+ Infinitive Stem +* **-t** *or* -**et**

spielen	*ge* + **spiel** + *t* = **gespielt**
lachen	*ge* + **lach** + *t* = **gelacht**

Past participle of strong verbs

The past participle of most strong verbs is formed by placing the prefix **ge-** in front of the past participle stem and adding **-en** at the end of the stem.

Past Participle (Strong Verbs) = **ge-** + *Past Participle Stem* + **-en**

singen	*ge* + **sung** + *en* = **gesungen**

As we know, strong verbs are characterized by a stem vowel change in the past tense. The past participle also reflects this characteristic. **However, the stem vowel of the past participle can be the same as the stem vowel in the simple past, as the stem vowel in the infinitive, or a different vowel altogether.** Thus, although there are some basic sound patterns that help predict these changes, it is necessary to learn the principal parts for each new strong verb.

Regular Weak Verbs

The present perfect tense of most regular weak verbs is formed with the present tense of **haben** or **sein** and the past participle of the main verb. Study the following forms:

Verb	*Third Person Singular*	*Past Participle*
arbeiten	**er arbeitet**	**gearbeitet**
lieben	**er liebt**	**geliebt**
machen	**er macht**	**gemacht**
öffnen	**er öffnet**	**geöffnet**

Wir *haben* **einen Wagen** *gekauft.*	*We bought a car.*
Er *hat* **die Wahrheit** *gesagt.*	*He told the truth.*
Ich *habe* **den Lehrer** *gefragt.*	*I asked the teacher.*
Habt *ihr* **auch** *gearbeitet?*	*Did you also work?*

Weak Verbs without the **ge-** *Prefix*

The past participle of weak verbs ending in **-ieren** does not take the ge- prefix.

Infinitive	Past Participle
probieren	**probiert**
studieren	**studiert**
telefonieren	**telefoniert**

Don't Forget

Additional verbs without **ge-** *prefix*

Weak or strong verbs with the following inseparable prefixes do not take the additional **ge-** prefix in the past participle: **be-, emp-, ent-, er-, ge-, ver-, zer-** (see section on inseparable prefix verbs).

Weak Verbs		*Strong Verbs*	
Infinitive	*Past Participle*	*Infinitive*	*Past Participle*
bestellen	**bestellt**	**bestehen**	**bestanden**
entdecken	**entdeckt**	**entnehmen**	**entnommen**
erklären	**erklärt**	**erfahren**	**erfahren**
gehören	**gehört**	**gefallen**	**gefallen**
verkaufen	**verkauft**	**verbergen**	**verborgen**

Irregular Weak Verbs

The past participles of the irregular weak verbs also have a stem vowel change.

Infinitive		*Simple Past*	*Past Participle*
brennen	*to burn*	brannte	*gebrannt*
bringen	*to bring*	brachte	*gebracht*
denken	*to think*	dachte	*gedacht*
kennen	*to know (a person)*	kannte	*gekannt*
nennen	*to name*	nannte	*genannt*
senden	*to send*	sandte	*gesandt*
wenden	*to turn*	wandte	*gewandt*
wissen	*to know (a fact)*	wußte	*gewußt*

Intransitive Verbs

The present perfect tense of some German verbs is formed with the present tense of the auxiliary verb **sein** instead of **haben**. These are intransitive verbs that denote a change of location or condition.

Infinitive		Past Participle
begegnen	to meet	**ist begegnet**
klettern	to climb	**ist geklettert**
reisen	to travel	**ist gereist**
wandern	to wander, hike	**ist gewandert**

Ich *bin* **auf den Baum** *geklettert.*	*I climbed the tree.*
Er *ist* **nach Deutschland** *gereist.*	*He traveled to Germany.*

Strong Verbs

The present perfect tense of strong verbs is formed with the present tense of **haben** or **sein** and the past participle of the main verb. Remember also that the past participle may have a vowel change, and that the inseparable prefixes do not take the **ge-** prefix.

Past Participles With No Vowel Change

Infinitive		Simple Past	Past Participle
essen	to eat	aß	**gegessen**
fahren	to drive, go	fuhr	**(ist) gefahren**
fallen	to fall	fiel	**(ist) gefallen**
fangen	to catch	fing	**gefangen**
geben	to give	gab	**gegeben**
halten	to stop, hold	hielt	**gehalten**
kommen	to come	kam	**(ist) gekommen**
lassen	to let	ließ	**gelassen**
laufen	to run	lief	**(ist) gelaufen**
lesen	to read	las	**gelesen**
schlafen	to sleep	schlief	**geschlafen**
schlagen	to hit	schlug	**geschlagen**
sehen	to see	sah	**gesehen**
tragen	to carry, wear	trug	**getragen**

treten	to step	trat	(ist) getreten
vergessen	to forget	vergaß	vergessen
wachsen	to grow	wuchs	(ist) gewachsen

Remember!

The past participles preceded by **ist** take **sein** as the auxiliary verb in the present perfect tense.

Er *ist* **nach Hamburg** *gefahren.*
   He went (by car or train) to Hamburg.
Ich *bin* **ins Zimmer** *getreten.*
   I stepped into the room.
Wir *sind* **gestern** *gekommen.*
   We came yesterday.

Past Participles with Vowel Change

Many strong verbs change their stem in the past participle. The following groups may facilitate learning these past participles.

Changes from **ei** *to* **ie, i**

Infinitive		Simple Past	Past Participle
	ei	*ie*	*ie*
bleiben	*to stay*	blieb	(ist) geblieben
scheinen	*to shine, seem*	schien	geschienen
schreiben	*to write*	schrieb	geschrieben
schweigen	*to be silent*	schwieg	geschwiegen
steigen	*to climg*	stieg	(ist) gestiegen
	ei	*i*	*i*
beißen	*to bite*	biß	gebissen
leiden	*to suffer*	litt	gelitten

reiten	to ride	ritt	(ist) geritten
schneiden	to cut	schnitt	geschnitten

Changes from ie, au to o, e

Infinitive		Simple Past	Past Participle
ie		*o*	*o*
fliegen	to fly	flog	(ist) geflogen
fließen	to flow	floß	(ist) geflossen
frieren	to freeze	fror	gefroren
riechen	to smell	roch	gerochen
schießen	to shoot	schoß	geschossen
schließen	to close, shut	schloß	geschlossen
verlieren	to lose	verlor	verloren
ziehen	to pull	zog	gezogen

au		*o*	*o*
saufen	to drink (animals)	soff	gesoffen

ie		*a*	*e*
liegen	to lie	lag	gelegen

Changes from i to u, o, e

Infinitive		Simple Past	Past Participle
i		*a*	*u*
binden	to bind	band	gebunden
finden	to find	fand	gefunden
singen	to sing	sang	gesungen
sinken	to sink	sank	(ist) gesunken
springen	to jump	sprang	(ist) gesprungen
stinken	to stink	stank	gestunken
trinken	to drink	trank	getrunken

i			*o*
beginnen	to begin	begann	begonnen
gewinnen	to win	gewann	gewonnen
schwimmen	to swim	schwamm	geschwommen

i			*e*
bitten	to ask	bat	gebeten

sitzen	*to sit*	saß	**gesessen**

Changes from **e, u** *to* **a, o**

Infinitive		*Simple Past*	*Past Participle*
e		*a*	*o*
brechen	*to break*	brach	**gebrochen**
empfehlen	*to recommend*	empfahl	**empfohlen**
helfen	*to help*	half	**geholfen**
nehmen	*to take*	nahm	**genommen**
sprechen	*to speak*	sprach	**gesprochen**
sterben	*to die*	starb	**(ist) gestorben**
treffen	*to meet*	traf	**getroffen**
werfen	*to throw*	warf	**geworfen**
e		*i*	*a*
gehen	*to go*	ging	**(ist) gegangen**
e		*a*	*a*
stehen	*to stand*	stand	**gestanden**
u		*a*	*a*
tun	*to do*	tat	**getan**

Auxiliary Verbs sein, haben, werden

The present perfect tense of **sein, haben, werden** is as follows:

sein	*haben*	*werden*
ich bin gewesen	**ich habe gehabt**	**ich bin geworden**
du bist gewesen	**du hast gehabt**	**du bist geworden**
er ist gewesen	**er hat gehabt**	**er ist geworden**
wir sind gewesen	**wir haben gehabt**	**wir sind geworden**
ihr seid gewesen	**ihr habt gehabt**	**ihr seid geworden**
sie sind gewesen	**sie haben gehabt**	**sie sind geworden**

Wir *sind* **in Nürnberg** *gewesen.*	*We were in Nürnberg.*
Ich *bin* **müde** *geworden.*	*I became tired.*
Hast **du Geld** *gehabt?*	*Did you have money?*

Past Perfect Tense

Weak and Strong Verbs

The past perfect tense, sometimes referred to as the *pluperfect,* of both weak and the strong verbs is formed with the simple past tense form of the auxiliary **haben** or **sein** plus the past participle.

> *Past Perfect = Simple Past Tense of* **sein** *or* **haben** *+ Past Participle*

Study the following forms:

ich hatte gesucht	**ich war gegangen**
du hattest gesucht	**du warst gegangen**
er hatte gesucht	**er war gegangen**
wir hatten gesucht	**wir waren gegangen**
ihr hattet gesucht	**ihr wart gegangen**
sie hatten gesucht	**sie waren gegangen**

Ich *hatte* **die Geschichte** *gehört.*	*I had heard the story.*
Wir *waren* **zu Hause** *geblieben.*	*We had stayed at home.*
Er *war* **schon dort** *gewesen.*	*He had already been there.*
Sie *hatten* **den Hund** *gefüttert.*	*They had fed the dog.*

In German, as in English, the past perfect tense usually occurs in the context of past tense narration, where it is used to report events that took place prior to another event in the past.

Future Tense

Weak and Strong Verbs

The future tense of both weak and strong verbs is formed with the auxiliary verb **werden** and the infinitive. The infinitive is in last position, unless it occurs in a dependent clause.

> *Future Tense = Present Tense of* **werden** + *Infinitive*

Study the following conjugation:

ich werde suchen	wir werden suchen
du wirst suchen	ihr werdet suchen
er wird suchen	sie werden suchen

Ich *werde* **dich nicht** *vergessen.*	*I shall not forget you.*
Werdet **ihr auch kommen?**	*Will you also come?*
Wir *werden* **einen Hund** *kaufen.*	*We are going to buy a dog.*

Use of the Future Tense

The future tense is of course used to indicate actions that will take place entirely in the future. If an adverb or phrase indicating future time is not expressed, the future using **werden** is commonly used. If the adverbial indicator is present or if it is obvious from the context that the future is clearly intended, the present tense (with a future meaning) is frequently encountered, particularly in spoken German.

Wir *werden* **dich** *besuchen.*	*We will visit you.*
Ich *fahre morgen* **nach Ulm.**	*I am going to Ulm tomorrow.*

Caution: The English modal verb *to want to* corresponds to the German *wollen,* which must not be confused with the future. **Ich** _will_ **nach Berlin fahren.** *I* _want to_ *drive to Berlin.* (See modal auxiliaries later in this chapter.)

Probability

In German the future tense may also indicate present or future probability or likelihood, particularly when used in conjunction with adverbs such as **sicher, schon, vielleicht, wohl.**

Die Wolken sind sehr dunkel. Es *wird wohl bald* **regnen.**
The clouds are very dark. It will probably rain soon.

Ingo ist nicht zur Schule gekommen. Er *wird sicher* **krank** *sein.*
Ingo didn't come to school. He's probably sick.

Du hast schwer gearbeitet. Du *wirst wohl* **müde** *sein.*
You've worked hard. You're probably tired.

Verbs with Inseparable Prefixes

Verbs beginning with the prefixes **be-, emp-, ent-, er-, ge-, ver-, zer-** are called *inseparable prefix* verbs because these prefixes are never separated from the verb stem. The inseparable prefixes do not have an independent meaning by themselves and they cannot stand alone. They do, however, change the meaning of the stem verb to which they are prefixed.

The inseparable prefix verbs can be either strong or weak, following the same conjugational patterns of the verb stem, except that they do not take the characteristic **ge-** prefix in the past participle.

In spoken German the inseparable prefixes do not receive any stress. The primary stress is given to the first syllable of the verb stem. Only the prefix **zer-** has a constant meaning. It denotes destruction or reduction to small parts or components: **drücken** *(to squeeze),* **zerdrücken** *(to squash).*

Note how the different prefixes alter the meanings of the verbs.

stehen - *to stand*

bestehen	*to pass*	**Ich** *habe* **das Examen** *bestanden.* (the prefix *be* usually makes the verb transitive)
entstehen	*to originate*	**Wie** *entsteht* **das Gas?**
gestehen	*to confess*	**Er** *gestand* **das Verbrechen** *(crime).*
verstehen	*to understand*	**Sie** *werden* **das Problem** *verstehen.*

fallen - *to fall*

gefallen	*to be pleasing*	**Das Kleid** *hat* **ihr** *gefallen.*
verfallen	*to decline*	*Verfällt* **das Zentrum?**
zerfallen	*to fall apart*	**Der Kuchen** *ist zerfallen.*

Verbs with Separable Prefixes

Another group of verbs is called the *separable prefix verbs* because the prefix is separated from the verb stem under certain conditions. Many separable prefixes are prepositions (**an, auf, nach**) or adverbs (**zurück, heim, vorbei**); others are verbs (**kennen, spazieren, stehen**). Occasionally adjectives and nouns also function as separable prefixes. The separable prefixes have definite meanings, very often denoting direction. However, not all German prefixes can be translated into idiomatic English by using these equivalents

Like the inseparable prefix verbs, the separable prefix verbs can be either strong or weak. However, in forming the past participle they add the prefix **ge-** in addition to the separable prefix.

Unlike the inseparable prefix verbs, the separable prefix verbs always have their main stress on the prefix. Here are some examples.

ab	*off, down*	**abfliegen** *(to take off)*
auf	*up, open*	**aufstehen** *(to get up)*
fort	*away*	**fortgehen** *(to go away)*
heim	*home*	**heimkommen** *(to come home)*
mit	*with, along*	**mitfahren** *(to ride along)*
zurück	*back*	**zurücknehmen** *(to take back)*
zusammen	*together*	**zusammenkommen** *(to come together)*

Position of the Separable Prefix

A separable prefix is always the final element of the sentence or main clause when the verb is in the present tense, the simple past tense, or the imperative. Study the following examples.

Present Tense
   Ich *gehe oft* **aus.**
   Kommst **du auch** *heim?*
   Geht **ihr morgen** *mit?*

Simple Past Tense
   Sie *ging* **abends** *spazieren.*
   Warum *schaute* **sie es** *an?*

Imperative

> *Geh* **mit uns** *spazieren!*
> *Kommt* **bald** *zurück!*
> *Lernen* **Sie Arnold** *kennen!*
> (See the section on the imperative later in this chapter)

Infinitive

The separable prefix does not separate from the verb stem in the infinitive. However, in infinitive clauses with **zu,** the **zu** comes between the separable prefix and the verb stem.

> **Ich bin bereit** *anzufangen.*   *I am ready to start.*

Compound Tenses

<u>Future Tense</u>

> **Er** *wird* **wohl** *mitessen.*
> **Ich** *werde* **nicht** *ausgehen.*

<u>Present and Past Perfect Tense</u>

Note that the separable prefix verbs take the **ge-** prefix. However, it is placed between the separable prefix and the past participle stem.

> **Der Zug** *ist* **endlich** *ange*kommen.
> **Mutter** *hat* **schon** *einge*kauft.
> **Sie** *waren* **schon** *ange*kommen.
> **Der Lehrer** *hatte* **das Licht** *ange*macht.

Separable Prefix Verbs in Dependent Clauses

The separable prefix does not separate from the verb when it occurs in a dependent clause. Study the following.

Present	**Ich weiß, daß er bald** *ankommt.*
Simple Past	**Sie lachte, als ich** *hinfiel.*
Future	**Er weiß, warum ich** *mitgehen werde.*
Present Perfect	**Ich freue mich, daß du** *heimgekommen bist.*

Reflexive Verbs

A reflexive verb shows that the action of the verb is both performed and received by the subject, i.e., the object of the verb is identical with the subject of the verb. *He amuses himself easily.* The object pronoun used to show this relationship is called a reflexive pronoun because it refers or reflects back to the subject of the sentence or clause. In English this relationship is often just implied. *He is shaving (himself).* In German such verbs require a reflexive pronoun (**Er rasiert sich.** *He is shaving.*) Other verbs may be used both reflexively (**Er amüsiert sich leicht.** *He amuses himself easily.*) and nonreflexively (**Er amüsiert sein Enkelkind.** *He amuses his grandchild.*)

You Should Know

In German reflexive pronouns may be in either the accusative or the dative case, depending on how the reflexive pronoun functions within the sentence. When the reflexive pronoun functions as a direct object, the accusative is generally used.

Reflexive Verbs Governing the Accusative Case

The following is a partial list of common reflexive verbs followed by accusative reflexive pronouns.

sich anziehen	*to dress*	**sich gewöhnen an**	*to get used to*
sich aufregen	*to get excited*	**sich interessieren für**	
			to be interested in
sich bewegen	*to move*	**sich rasieren**	*to shave*
sich entscheiden	*to decide*	**sich setzen**	*to sit down*
sich entschuldigen		**sich verletzen**	*to hurt oneself*
to apologize, excuse oneself			
sich erinnern an	*to remember*	**sich verspäten**	*to be late*
sich erkälten	*to catch a cold*	**sich vorstellen**	
			to introduce oneself
sich freuen	*to be happy*	**sich waschen**	*to wash oneself*

Accusative Reflexive Pronouns

	ACCUSATIVE CASE		
	Personal Pronouns	*Reflexive Pronouns*	
ich	mich	mich	*myself*
du	dich	dich	*yourself*
er	ihn	sich	*himself*
sie	sie	sich	*herself*
es	es	sich	*itself*
wir	uns	uns	*ourselves*
ihr	euch	euch	*yourselves*
sie	sie	sich	*themselves*
Sie	Sie	sich	*yourselves*

Note that **sich** (reflexive pronoun for **Sie**) is not capitalized.

Er *interessiert sich* **für klassische Musik.**
Erinnern **Sie** *sich* **an die alte Heimat?**
Wir *legten uns* **aufs Sofa.**

The reflexive pronoun is placed as close as possible to the subject. However, it never comes between pronoun subject and verb.

Reflexive Verbs Governing the Dative Case

When the verb has a direct object in the accusative case, the reflexive pronoun, which functions like an indirect object, is in the dative case. Note the difference between the two constructions below.

Accusative reflexive pronoun	**Ich wasche** *mich.*	*I wash (myself).*
Dative reflexive pronoun	**Ich wasche** *mir die Hände.*	*I wash my hands.*

Dative Reflexive Pronouns

	DATIVE CASE		
Personal Pronouns		*Reflexive Pronouns*	
ich	**mir**	**mir**	*myself*
du	**dir**	**dir**	*yourself*
er	**ihm**	**sich**	*himself*
sie	**ihr**	**sich**	*herself*
es	**ihm**	**sich**	*itself*
wir	**uns**	**uns**	*ourselves*
ihr	**euch**	**euch**	*yourselves*
sie	**sie**	**sich**	*themselves*
Sie	**Sie**	**sich**	*yourselves*

The dative reflexive pronoun is also frequently used with such verbs as **kaufen, holen, bestellen, machen, nehmen.**

Ich *kaufte mir* **ein Auto.**	*I bought (for) myself a car.*
Er *holt sich* **etwas.**	*He's getting something for himself.*

Dative Reflexive Pronouns with Parts of the Body

To show possession when referring to parts of the body or articles of clothing, German often uses the definite article with a dative reflexive in place of the possessive adjective.

Ich *putze mir* **die Zähne.**	*I am brushing my teeth.*
Ziehst **du** *dir* **die Schuhe an?**	*Are you putting on your shoes?*
Er *wäscht sich* **die Haare.**	*He's washing his hair.*

Modal Auxiliary Verbs

The modal auxiliaries do not by themselves express an action, process, or change in condition, but instead affect the meaning of the main verb.

It is often said that they indicate an attitude toward the main verb. The modal auxiliaries and their basic meanings are:

dürfen	permission	*may, to be allowed to*
	negative—prohibition	*must* NOT
müssen	necessity, obligation	*must, to have to*
können	ability	*can, to be able to, know how to*
mögen	inclination, desire	*to like to, want to,*
	negative—not liking	NOT *to like to, want to*

mögen inclination, desire | to like to, want to,
negative—not liking NOT *to like to, want to*
Note: In everyday speech, the subjunctive form of *mögen, möchten,* is usually used. (*Ich möchte gehen.* I would like to go) To express the past, the verb *wollen* is used (*Ich wollte gehen.* I wanted to go).

wollen	desire, intention	*to want to*
sollen	obligation	*should, to be supposed to*

Present Tense

The present tense of the modal auxiliary verbs is irregular. Study the following forms:

dürfen		*müssen*	
ich darf	**wir dürfen**	**ich muß**	**wir müssen**
du darfst	**ihr dürft**	**du mußt**	**ihr müßt**
er darf	**sie dürfen**	**er muß**	**sie müssen**
können		*mögen*	
ich kann	**wir können**	**ich mag**	**wir mögen**
du kannst	**ihr könnt**	**du magst**	**ihr mögt**
er kann	**sie können**	**er mag**	**sie mögen**
wollen		*sollen*	
ich will	**wir wollen**	**ich soll**	**wir sollen**
du willst	**ihr wollt**	**du sollst**	**ihr sollt**
er will	**sie wollen**	**er soll**	**sie sollen**

Note that all modals except **sollen** use different stem vowels for the singular and the plural in the present tense. The first and third person singular forms have no personal endings in the present tense. The modal auxiliary verbs are used with the infinitive, which occurs in last position in the sentence, unless the modal plus infinitive is used in a dependent clause. In a negative sentence, **nicht** usually precedes the infinitive.

Darfst **du** *rauchen?*	*Are you allowed to smoke?*
Ihr *dürft nicht bleiben.*	*You must not stay.*
Ich *muß* **nach Hause** *gehen.*	*I have to go home.*
Werner *kann* **gut** *singen.*	*Werner can sing well.*
Ich *mag* **es auch** *hören.*	*I like to hear it also.*
Er *will* **es** *nicht machen.*	*He doesn't want to do it.*
Du *sollst* **die Wahrheit** *sagen.*	*You ought to tell the truth.*

Omission of the Dependent Infinitive with Modal Auxiliaries

In colloquial German the dependent infinitive is often omitted when the meaning of the sentence is clear from the context. This occurs most frequently with verbs such as **machen, tun** and with verbs of motion.

Er *muß* **nach Hause.**	*He has to go home.*
Mußt **du zur Arbeit?**	*Do you have to go to work?*
Gerda *kann* **Deutsch.**	*Gerda knows German.*
Wir *wollen* **ins Kino.**	*We want to go to the movies.*

Simple Past Tense

The simple past tense of the modals is formed by taking the infinitive stem, dropping the umlaut if there is one, and adding the past tense marker **-t** plus the past tense weak verb personal endings:

dürfen		*müssen*	
ich durfte	wir durften	ich mußte	wir mußten
du durftest	ihr durftet	du mußtest	ihr mußtet
er durfte	sie durften	er mußte	sie mußten
können		*mögen*	
ich konnte	wir konnten	ich mochte	wir mochten
du konntest	ihr konntet	du mochtest	ihr mochtet

er konnte	sie konnten	er mochte	sie mochten
wollen		*sollen*	
ich wollte	wir wollten	ich sollte	wir sollten
du wolltest	ihr wolltet	du solltest	ihr solltet
er wollte	sie wollten	er sollte	sie sollten

Wir *konnten* **die Geschichte nicht verstehen.**
Maria *durfte* **heute nicht mitkommen.**
Ich *mußte* **ihn tragen.**

Present and Past Perfect Tense

When no dependent infinitive is needed to convey the meaning in context, the following past participles of the modals are used.

dürfen	gedurft	müssen	gemußt
können	gekonnt	sollen	gesollt
mögen	gemocht	wollen	gewollt

Ich *habe* **Deutsch** *gekonnt.*	*I knew German.*
Sie *hat* **nach Hause** *gemußt.*	*She had to go home.*
Er *hatte* **Deutsch** *gekonnt.*	*He had known German.*

When the modal is followed by the infinitive of another verb, the present and past perfect are formed with a form of **haben** or **hatte**. The past participle is replaced by an infinitive form of the verb to which the infinitive from the modal is added. This construction is called the *double infinitive construction*, because the two infinitives occur together in last position in the sentence.

Sie *haben* **es nicht** *sehen dürfen.*	*They weren't allowed to see it.*
Ich *habe* **nicht** *arbeiten können.*	*I was not able to work.*
Er *hatte* **es** *machen müssen.*	*He had had to do it.*

Future Tense

The future of modals is formed with a form of **werden** plus the infinitive and the infinitive of the modal.

Er *wird* **wohl fahren** *können.*	*He'll probably be able to go.*
Ich *werde* **nicht** *kommen dürfen.*	*I will not be allowed to come.*

The Imperative

The imperative expresses commands, requests, or orders. Just as there are three different forms of address (**Sie, ihr, du**), there are three corresponding imperative forms. The imperative verb is the first element in a command, unless it is preceded by **bitte** (*please*). **Bitte** can also occur within the sentence or in last position. The word **doch** softens the command, corresponding to the English *why don't you?* In written German commands, an exclamation point is used.

Imperative = (**Bitte**) *Verb* + *(Personal Pronoun if Required)*

Study the examples of the imperative forms below:

Sie	**Spielen Sie!**	**Helfen Sie mir!**
ihr	**Spielt!**	**Helft mir!**
du	**Spiel(e)!**	**Hilf mir!**

The formal commands are formed by using the infinitive plus **Sie**. The pronoun **Sie** is always expressed.

Kommen Sie!	*Come.*
Bitte *parken Sie* **hier!**	*Please park here.*
Antworten Sie **doch!**	*Why don't you answer?*

The familiar plural command corresponds to the **ihr** form of the present tense. Note that the pronoun **ihr** is not expressed.

Macht **die Aufgaben!**	*Do your homework.*
Lest **doch den Roman!**	*Why don't you read the novel?*
Bitte *holt* **die Bücher!**	*Please get the books.*

The familiar singular command is formed from the infinitive stem plus **-e.** In colloquial speech this **-e** is often dropped (except in the cases noted below). Note that the pronoun **du** is not expressed.

Frag **deinen Vater!**	*Ask your father.*
Trink **doch Wasser!**	*Why don't you drink water?*
Such **das Bild bitte!**	*Look for the picture, please.*

When the infinitive stem ends in **-d, -t, -ig** or **-m, -n** preceded by a consonant other than **-l** or **-r**, the **-e** ending is not dropped.

Öffne **die Tür!**	*Open the door.*
Antworte **bitte!**	*Answer, please.*
Entschuldige **bitte!**	*Excuse me, please.*

Stem vowel **e** *changes to* **i** *or* **ie**

Strong verbs with a stem vowel change in the present tense from **e** to **i** or **ie** have the same change in the familiar singular imperative.

Gib **Gisela den Brief!**	*Give the letter to Gisela.*
Hilf **uns!**	*Help us.*
Lies **doch das Buch!**	*Why don't you read the book?*

The imperative forms of **haben, sein, werden, wissen** are slightly irregular. Study the following forms:

	Formal	Familiar Plural	Familiar Singular
haben	**Haben Sie!**	**Habt!**	**Hab(e)!**
sein	**Seien Sie!**	**Seid!**	**Sei!**
werden	**Werden Sie!**	**Werdet!**	**Werde!**
wissen	**Wissen Sie!**	**Wißt!**	**Wisse!**

Remember!

Reflexive Imperative Forms

The reflexive pronouns are always expressed in commands. The reflexive pronoun follows the imperative form of the verb.

Setz *dich!*   **Zieht** *euch* **um!**
Fürchten *Sie sich* **nicht!**   **Waschen wir** *uns!*

First Person Command (*Let's*)

The idea of *let's* is expressed by using the first person plural. The pronoun **wir** follows the conjugated verb.

Singen wir!	*Let's sing.*
Fahren wir **mit dem Auto!**	*Let's go by car.*

The Conditional and Subjunctive

The Conditional

The German conditional is formed with the auxiliary **würden** plus infinitive and corresponds to the English verb pattern *would* plus infinitive. The conditional expresses what would happen if it were not for another circumstance. The infinitive of the conditional is in last position, unless it occurs in a dependent clause. Study the following:

Ich würde sagen	**wir würden sagen**
du würdest sagen	**ihr würdet sagen**
er würde sagen	**sie würden sagen**

Ich *würde* **dem Kind** *helfen.*	*I would help the child.*
Würdest **du das Geld nehmen?**	*Would you take the money?*
Er weiß, daß ich es *sagen würde.*	*He knows that I would say it.*

In both English and German the conditional is used in the conclusion of contrary-to-fact *if* clauses. It is used increasingly in place of the subjunctive in the conclusion of the condition in spoken and informal German. (See the section on the subjunctive.)

The conditional is also used as a polite form of request.

Würden **Sie bitte** *warten?*	*Would you please wait?*
Würdest **du mir bitte** *helfen?*	*Would you please help me?*

The Subjunctive

Whereas the *indicative mood* is used to make statements of fact, ask questions, and generally describe reality, the *subjunctive mood* is used in referring to conditions and situations that are contrary to fact, unlikely, uncertain or hypothetical. For example, the indicative is used for actions that have taken place, are taking place, or will very likely take place.

Er hat großen Hunger.	*He is very hungry.*
Ich weiß, daß sie krank ist.	*I know that she is ill.*
Er hat es genommen.	*He took it.*

The subjunctive is used to express that a certain action has not or may not take place, because it is a supposition, conjecture, or desire, rather than a fact.

Ich wollte, er *wäre* **hier!**	*I wish he were here.*
Er sagte, er *würde* **kommen.**	*He said he would come.*
Sie tut, als ob sie Geld *hätte.*	*She acts as if she had money.*

General Subjunctive

The general subjunctive is often referred to as *subjunctive II* because it is based on the simple past tense, the second principle part of the verb. The uses of the general subjunctive fall into four main categories:

 **Note!**

(1) Wishes
(2) Contrary-to-fact conditions
(3) Hypothetical statements and questions
(4) Polite requests and questions

Present-Time Subjunctive

In the subjunctive, we do not speak of tenses, but rather of the time (either present and future or past) to which the statement applies. The present-time subjunctive is used to refer to wishes, unreal conditions, and hypothetical events in the present or future. It is formed by adding the subjunctive personal endings to the stem of the simple past. For the past stem, just drop the **-en** from the simple past tense of the first person plural. This applies to both strong and weak verbs.

Present-Time Subjunctive = Past Stem + Subjunctive Personal Ending

The subjunctive personal endings are as follows:

	Singular	*Plural*
First Person	**-e**	**-en**
Second Person	**-est**	**-et**
Third Person	**-e**	**-en**

Thus the fully conjugated present-time subjunctive for **sagen** is:

ich sagte	**wir sagten**
du sagtest	**ihr sagtet**
er sagte	**sie sagten**

Weak Verbs

The present-time subjunctive of weak verbs is identical with the simple past indicative. This is also true in English, where the present-time subjunctive of all verbs, except *to be*, is identical with the past indicative: *If* I had *money* . . . ; *If* he *lost* everything . . . ; but: *If* we were *rich*. . . .

In English, as well as in German, these present-time subjunctive forms are ambiguous. Only the context makes clear whether the forms are used in the past indicative or the present subjunctive. For this reason the present conditional **würden** plus infinitive is often substituted for the subjunctive in German. (See section on the conditional.) The German present-time subjunctive corresponds to the English present conditional *would* plus infinitive (*would run*) or to the present-time subjunctive (*ran*), depending on use. Although the present-time subjunctive looks like the simple past indicative, it always refers to present or future time.

Irregular Weak Verbs

Bringen, denken, wissen add an umlaut to the simple past stems plus the subjunctive endings to form the present-time subjunctive.

ich brächte	ich dächte	ich wüßte
du brächtest	du dächtest	du wüßtest
er brächte	er dächte	er wüßte
wir brächten	wir dächten	wir wüßten
ihr brächtet	ihr dächtet	ihr wüßtet
sie brächten	sie dächten	sie wüßten

Ich *wünschte,* **er** *dächte* **daran.**	*I wish he would think of it.*
Ich *wünschte,* **wlr** *wüßten* **es.**	*I wish we would know it.*

Strong Verbs

The present-time subjunctive of strong verbs is also formed by adding the subjunctive endings to the simple past tense stems. However, those verbs containing the vowels **a, o, u** add an umlaut.

No Umlaut		*Umlaut*	
ich bliebe	wir blieben	ich nähme	wir nähmen
du bliebest	ihr bliebet	du nähmest	ihr nähmet
er bliebe	sie blieben	er nähme	sie nähmen
Umlaut		*Umlaut*	
ich flöge	wir flögen	ich führe	wir führen
du flögest	ihr flöget	du führest	ihr führet
er flöge	sie flögen	er führe	sie führen

Ich *wünschte,* **er** *käme* **heute.**	*I wish he would come today.*
Ich *wünschte,* **du** *gingest* **jetzt.**	*I wish you would go now.*

Auxiliaries *haben* and *sein*

Study the following:

ich hätte	wir hätten	ich wäre	wir wären
du hättest	ihr hättet	du wärest	ihr wäret
er hätte	sie hätten	er wäre	sie wären

Wenn ich nur Zeit *hätte!*		*If only I had money.*
Wenn sie nur hier *wäre!*		*If only she were here.*

Modal Verbs

Modal auxiliary verbs retain the vowels of the infinitive in the stems of the present-time subjunctive. Note the change in **mögen**.

dürfen	**ich dürfte**	*might, would be permitted, may I?*
können	**ich könnte**	*were able, would be able*
mögen	**ich möchte**	*would like*
müssen	**ich müßte**	*ought to, would have to*
sollen	**ich sollte**	*should, would have to*
wollen	**ich wollte**	*wanted, would want to*

The subjunctive form of the modals is frequently used to express possibility or opinions and to phrase politely. In English the modals are usually expressed with *would* plus the meaning of the modal.

Du *solltest* **zu Hause bleiben.**	*You should stay at home.*
Möchtest **du eine Tasse Tee?**	*Would you like a cup of tea?*
Dürfte **ich es sehen?**	*Could I see it?*

Wishes

Contrary-to-fact wishes

With a contrary-to-fact wish, the speaker expresses his or her dissatisfaction with an actual situation and expresses how he or she would like it to be. Such wishes may be introduced by the present-time subjunctive of verbs of wishing, e.g., **ich wollte, ich wünschte.**

Fact	**Er ist nicht zu Hause**	*He is not at home.*
Wish	*Ich wollte,* **er wäre zu Hause.**	*I wish he were home.*

Contrary-to-fact wishes introduced by **wenn** *(if)*

When the contrary-to-fact wish is expressed within a **wenn** *(if)* clause, the conjugated verb is in last position, as is required in dependent clauses. Such wishes often contain the words **nur** or **doch**, corresponding to English *only*.

Wenn sie nur daran *glaubten!*	*If only they believed in it.*
Wenn er doch nicht *rauchte!*	*If only he wouldn't smoke.*
Wenn ich es nur tun *dürfte!*	*If only I were allowed to do it.*

Contrary-to-fact wishes not introduced by **wenn**

The introductory **wenn** of the preceding wishes can also be omitted. In that case the conjugated verb is in first position.

Hätte **ich nur mehr Zeit!**	*If only I had more time.*
Gäbe **es nur besseres Essen!**	*If only there were better food.*
Dürfte **ich nur heim gehen!**	*If only I could go home.*

Clauses Introduced by **als ob**

The subjunctive is used in clauses introduced by **als ob** or **als wenn** (as if) because the speaker makes an unreal comparison. If the word **ob** is omitted, then the verb follows **als.**

Er sieht aus, **als ob** *er krank wäre.*	*He looks as if he were ill.*
Sie tun, **als** *hätten sie Angst.*	*They act as if they were afraid.*

Conditional Sentences

Conditional sentences consist of a conditional clause, introduced by **wenn,** and a conclusion. The verbs in a conditional sentence may be in the indicative or the subjunctive mood. If the speaker wants to express that the condition is factual, real, or fulfillable, the indicative is used.

> **Wenn ich Geld** *habe, kaufe* **ich es.** *If have money, I'll buy it.*
> *When I have money, I'll buy it.*

In this sentence, the speaker does not yet have money, but there is a good probability that he or she will have it in the future.

If a condition is contrary to fact, unreal, or unfulfillable, the subjunctive is used.

> **Wenn ich Geld** *hätte, kaufte* **ich es.** *If I had money, I would buy it.*

With the use of the subjunctive mood of the verb, the speaker expresses that he or she does not have the money now, nor is he or she likely to have it in the future. In the preceding sentence, the present-time subjunctive was used in both the condition and the conclusion. Variations from the above patterns are possible in German. The present conditional (the verb **würde** plus infinitive) is frequently used to replace the ambiguous subjunctive form of weak verbs and increasingly of strong verbs as well.

Wenn ich reich *wäre,*	*machte* **ich eine Weltreise.** or *würde* **ich eine Weltreise machen.**

Wenn es kälter *wäre,*	*zöge* **ich den Pelzmantel an.** or *würde* **ich den Pelzmantel** *anziehen.*

The present-time subjunctive of **haben, sein,** and the modal verbs is not replaced by the present conditional. In other words, **hätte, wäre,** etc. are used instead of **würde** plus the infinitive.

The conjugated verb is in first position when **wenn** is omitted.

Wäre **das Radio kaputt, (dann)** *würde* **sie es** *reparieren.*
If the radio were broken, (then) she would fix it.

Machtest **du das Fenster** *zu,* **(dann)** *wäre* **es nicht so kalt.**
If you closed the window, (then) it wouldn't be so cold.

Past-Time Subjunctive

The past-time subjunctive is used to refer to wishes, unreal conditions, and hypothetical events relating to any time in the past. It is formed with **hätte** or **wäre** plus the past participle.

> *Past-Time Subjunctive =*
> **hätte** *or* **wäre** + *Past Participle*

The German past-time subjunctive corresponds to the English *had* plus participle (*had run, had gone*) or to *would* plus *have* and the past participle (*would have run, would have gone*).

Wenn sie nur *mitgeholfen hätte!*	*If only she had helped out.*
Hätte **ich nur den Film** *gesehen!*	*If only I had seen the film.*

> **Wenn wir** *gelernt hätten, hätten*   *If we had studied, we would*
> **wir die Antworten** *gewußt.*   *have known the answers.*

Passive Voice

The passive voice in German consists of a form of **werden** plus the past participle of the main verb. In German, as in English, passive constructions shift the emphasis from the subject of the active sentence to the direct object. What had been the direct object of the active sentence becomes the subject of the passive sentence. In an active sentence the subject performs an action, whereas in a passive sentence the subject is acted upon by an agent that was the subject of the active sentence. This agent might or might not be expressed in the passive. If the agent is expressed, it is preceded by **von** (+ dative) if it is a person; if the agent is an impersonal means by which something is done, it is preceded by **durch** (+ accusative). In English *by* is used for both.

Active
> **Die Eltern fragen den Jungen.**   *The parents ask the boy.*

Passive
> **Der Junge** *wird von den Eltern gefragt.*   *The boy is asked by his parents.*

Active
> **Feuer zerstört das Haus.**   *Fire is destroying the house.*

Passive
> **Das Haus** *wird durch Feuer zerstört.*   *The house is destroyed by fire.*

However, many passive sentences in German do not express an agent. They simply consist of a subject and the passive verb pattern.

> **Die Tür** *wird geschlossen.*   *The door is (being) closed.*
> **Die Vorlesung** *wird gehalten.*   *The lecture is (being) held.*

Present Tense

The present tense of the passive is constructed from the present tense of **werden** plus the past participle of the main verb.

> *Present Tense of Passive = Present Tense of* **werden** + *Past Participle*

Study the following:

ich werde gefragt	**wir werden gefragt**
du wirst gefragt	**ihr werdet gefragt**
er wird gefragt	**sie werden gefragt**

Past Tense

The simple past tense of the passive is constructed from the past tense of **werden** plus the past participle of the main verb.

> *Past Tense of Passive = Past Tense of* **werden** + *Past Participle*

ich wurde gefragt	**wir wurden gefragt**
du wurdest gefragt	**ihr wurdet gefragt**
er wurde gefragt	**sie wurden gefragt**

Wir *wurden* **von ihm** *gesehen.*   *We were seen by him.*
Das Auto *wurde repariert.*   *The car was repaired.*

Present Perfect and Past Perfect

The simple present tense and the simple past tense of **sein** are used to form the present perfect and past perfect passive. The **-ge** prefix is dropped from the past participle **geworden** in the passive.

> *Present Perfect Passive = Present Tense of* **sein** + *Past Participle of Main Verb* + **worden**

ich bin gefragt worden	**wir sind gefragt worden**
du bist gefragt worden	**ihr seid gefragt worden**
er ist gefragt worden	**sie sind gefragt worden**

> *Past Perfect Passive = Past Tense of* **sein** + *Past Participle of Main Verb* + **worden**

ich war gefragt worden	wir waren gefragt worden
du warst gefragt worden	ihr wart gefragt worden
er war gefragt worden	sie waren gefragt worden

Das Auto *ist* **vom Mechaniker** *repariert worden.*	*The car was repaired by the mechanic.*
Das Haus *war verkauft worden.*	*The house had been sold.*

Future Tense

The future passive is formed by the present tense of **werden** plus the past participle of the verb plus **werden**. It is used chiefly to express probability.

> *Future Passive = Present Tense of* **werden** + *Past Participle of Main Verb +* **werden**

ich werde gefragt werden	wir werden gefragt werden
du wirst gefragt werden	ihr werdet gefragt werden
er wird gefragt werden	sie werden gefragt werden

Er *wird* **wohl** *abgeholt werden.*	*He will probably be picked up.*
Die Äpfel *werden* **wohl** *gepflückt werden.*	*The apples will probably be picked.*

When an adverb of time referring to the future occurs in the sentence, the present passive is preferred.

Subtitute for the Passive

Spoken German prefers active constructions. Thus, there are ways of circumventing the passive. The most common method is to use a sentence containing the indefinite pronoun **man** (*one, we, you, they*) as the subject. Such sentences are often rendered as passive sentences in English. Compare the following:

Passive	**Ich** *bin gesehen worden.*	
Active	*Man hat* **mich** *gesehen.*	*I was seen.*

Passive	*Der Wagen wurde repariert.*
Active	*Man reparierte **den Wagen.** The car was repaired.*

> Note that the subject of the passive sentence becomes the direct object in the active sentence.

A Final Word of Caution

Do not confuse the following sentences for passive:

Das Geschäft ist geschlossen.
Der Wagen ist repariert.

Here the past participle is used as an adjective (*See* Chap. 5). This is <u>not</u> a passive construction, but simply describes a condition: *The store is closed; the car is fixed* (it is no longer in the shop). The passive sentences would read as follows:

Das Geschäft <u>wird</u> geschlossen.   *The store is being closed.*
Der Wagen <u>wird</u> repariert.   *The car is being repaired.*

Chapter 5
PRONOUNS

IN THIS CHAPTER:

✔ *Personal Pronouns*
✔ *Possessive Pronouns*
✔ *Demonstrative Pronouns*
✔ *Relative Pronouns*

Personal Pronouns

Nominative Case

Singular		Plural	
ich	*I*	**wir**	*we*
du	*you*	**ihr**	*you*
er	*he, it*	**sie**	*they*
es	*it*		
sie	*she, it*	**Sie**	*you*

In German there are three personal pronouns for *you*: a familiar singular (**du**), a familiar plural (**ihr**), and a formal form of address (**Sie**). The singular familiar pronoun **du** is used when addressing family members, close friends, children below the age of about sixteen, pets and other animals, and in prayer. The familiar plural **ihr** is used when addressing two or more members of these groups.

72

The familiar forms are also increasingly used among members of groups of equals, such as students, athletes, blue-collar workers, members of certain trades and occupations, soldiers, criminals, and in situations where first names are used.

The German pronoun of formal address **Sie** is used for acquaintances and other adults with whom the speaker is not on intimate terms, including anyone whom the speaker would address by last name or title. The **Sie** form is used for both the singular and the plural, and takes the same verb endings as the third person plural, **sie** (*they*). All forms of **Sie** and its possessive adjectives are always capitalized.

Karin, kannst *du* **mir helfen?**   *Karin, can* you *help me?*

Kinder, habt *ihr* **Zeit?**   *Children, do* you *have time?*

Frau Stifter, gehen *Sie* **auch?**   *Ms. Stifter, are* you *going also?*

The gender of a third person pronoun (**er, es, sie**) is determined by the gender of the word the pronoun refers back to. Masculine, feminine and neuter nouns are replaced by the masculine (**er**), feminine (**sie**), or neuter (**es**). When these pronouns refer to inanimate objects, they are translated by the English word *it*. The third person plural pronoun (**sie**) refers to both things and people and does not distinguish between masculine, feminine and neuter.

Wo ist der Wagen?   *Er* **ist in der Garage.**
Where is the car?   *It is in the garage.*

Wo ist der Junge?   *Er* **ist im Haus.**
Where is the boy?   *He is in the house.*

Wann kommt Mutter?   *Sie* **kommt bald.**
When is mother coming?   *She is coming soon.*

Wo sind die Bücher?   *Sie* **sind auf dem Schreibtisch.**
Where are the books?   *They are on the desk.*

Accusative Case

Singular		Plural	
mich	*me*	**uns**	*us*
dich	*you*	**euch**	*you*
ihn	*him, it*	**sie**	*them*
es	*it*		
sie	*her, it*	**Sie**	*you*

The accusative personal pronouns are used when they are the direct object of the verb or the object of a preposition requiring the accusative.

Er hat *mich* **besucht.**	*He visited* me.
Wir gehen ohne *ihn.*	*We are going without* him.
Liebst du *sie?*	*Do you love* her?

Dative Case

Singular		Plural	
mir	*me*	**uns**	*us*
dir	*you*	**euch**	*you*
ihm	*him, it*	**ihnen**	*them*
ihm	*it*		
ihr	*her, it*		
		Ihnen	*you*

The dative personal pronouns are used as the indirect object of verbs, or as the object of prepositions requiring the dative case.

Kaufst du *ihr* **etwas?**	*Are you buying* her *something?*
Warum ist er neben *dir?*	*Why is he beside* you?
Ich sage *Ihnen* **die Wahrheit.**	*I'm telling* you *the truth.*

Position of Pronoun Objects

With both a noun object and a pronoun object

When a sentence contains both a noun and a pronoun object, *the pronoun object precedes the noun object.*

Er hat *mir* **das Problem erklärt.**
Sie hat *es* **ihrem Vater erklärt.**

With two pronoun objects

When a sentence contains two pronouns objects, *the accusative pronoun always precedes the dative pronoun.*

Er hat *es* **mir erklärt.**
Sie hat *es* **ihm erklärt.**

Da-*compounds*

Third person pronouns used with prepositions refer only to people.

Sprecht ihr von Klaus?	**Ja, wir sprechen** *von ihm.*
	Yes, we're talking about him.
Wartet er auf seine Frau?	**Ja, er wartet** *auf sie.*
	Yes, he is waiting for her.

When the pronouns refer to things or ideas, **da-***compounds* are used. (*See* Chap. 8.)

Sprecht ihr von dem Plan?	**Ja, wir sprechen** *davon.*
	Yes, we are talking about it.
Wartest du auf den Brief?	**Ja, ich warte** *darauf.*
	Yes, I am waiting for it.

Remember!

Reflexive pronouns are used when the action of the verb is both executed by and performed upon the subject. A complete list and an explanation of reflexive pronouns and their use are given in Chap. 4.

Possessive Pronouns

mein-	*mine*	**unser-**	*ours*
dein-	*yours*	**eur-**	*yours*
sein-	*his, its*	**ihr-**	*theirs*
ihr-	*hers*		
		Ihr-	*yours*

The possessive pronoun receives the endings of **dieser, dieses, diese** in all cases. The gender of the possessive pronoun is determined by the gender of the noun it replaces.

Possessive used as adjective

Possessive used as pronoun

Wo hast du *deinen* **Hut verloren?**

Ich habe *meinen* **unterwegs verloren.**

Where did you lose your hat?

I lost mine along the way..

Das ist *sein* **Mantel.**

Meiner **hängt im Schrank.**

That is his coat.

Mine is hanging in the closet.

Demonstrative Pronouns

	Singular			Plural
	Masculine	*Neuter*	*Feminine*	*All Genders*
Nominative	**der**	**das**	**die**	**die**
	dieser	**dieses**	**diese**	**diese**
Accusative	**den**	**das**	**die**	**die**
	diesen	**dieses**	**diese**	**diese**
Dative	**dem**	**dem**	**der**	**denen**
	diesem	**diesem**	**dieser**	**diesen**

The demonstrative pronouns are used in place of the personal pronouns when the pronoun is to receive special emphasis. They follow the same pattern of case endings as the definite article, except that the form of the dative plural is **denen** instead of **den**. The noun it refers back to determines the gender and number of a demonstrative pronoun, and its case is determined by its function in the sentence.

In spoken German the demonstrative pronouns receive greater vocal stress and they are frequently expanded by the addition of **hier, da, dort** to more clearly specify the object referred to.

Ich kaufe *den hier.*	*I'll buy this one.*
Wem gehört *dieser dort?*	*To whom does that one belong?*
Geben Sie mir *diese da!*	*Give me those.*

Relative Pronouns

	Singular			*Plural*
	Masculine	*Neuter*	*Feminine*	*All Genders*
Nominative	**der**	**das**	**die**	**die**
Accusative	**den**	**das**	**die**	**die**
Dative	**dem**	**dem**	**der**	**denen**
Genitive	**dessen**	**dessen**	**deren**	**deren**

A relative pronoun both refers back to a previously mentioned noun or pronoun (its antecedent) and introduces a dependent relative clause that modifies this antecedent.

A relative clause must have the same number and gender as its antecedent. However, the grammatical case of a relative pronoun is determined by its function within the relative clause. Thus, if the relative pronoun is the subject of the relative clause, it must be in the nominative; if it is the direct object, it will be in the accusative, etc.

The relative pronoun will usually be the first element in the relative clause, although it will follow a preposition (see examples below).

Since the relative clause is a dependent (also called subordinate) clause, the conjugated verb moves to the final position in the clause. The relative clause is set off from the main clause by one or two commas. No contractions are possible with relative pronouns.

Nominative Case

Kennst du den Mann, *der* **dort steht?**
Do you know the man who is standing there?

Das Mädchen, *das* **in dem Geschäft arbeitet, ist seine Tochter.**
The girl who works in the store is his daughter.

Hier ist das Buch, *das* **er geschrieben hat.**
Here is the book that he wrote.

✷ Note!

Unlike English *(Here is the book he wrote),* the relative pronoun in German cannot be left out in any of the cases.

Accusative Case

The accusative case of the relative pronoun is used when it functions as the direct object of the verb or as the object of the preposition that governs the accusative.

Der Anzug, *den* **du trägst, ist altmodisch.**
The suit that you are wearing is old-fashioned.

Das Haus, in *das* **wir jetzt ziehen, ist hundert Jahre alt.**
The house into which we are moving is one hundred years old.

Dative Case

The dative relative pronouns are used when they function as the indirect object of the verb of the dependent clause, or when they are the object of verbs or prepositions requiring the dative.

Dort liegt der Hund, vor *dem* **ich Angst habe.**
There lies the dog I am afraid of (of which I am afraid).

Das Mädchen, *dem* **er die Kette gegeben hatte, hat sie verloren.**
The girl to whom I had given the necklace lost it.

Genitive Case

The genitive relative pronouns differ from the definite article and express the English *whose*.

Ich treffe meinen Freund, *dessen* **Auto ich brauche.**
I'll meet my friend whose car I need.

Dort ist die Dame, *deren* **Geld ich gefunden habe.**
There is the lady whose money I found.

Das Haus, *dessen* **Baustil mir gefällt, wurde 1910 gebaut.**
The house, the style of which I like, was built in 1910.

Indefinite Relative Pronouns

The indefinite relative pronouns **wer** (*whoever*) and **was** (*whatever*) are used when there is no antecedent. The case of **wer** is determined by its function in the relative clause. **Wer** is always singular.

Nominative	**wer**
Accusative	**wen**
Dative	**wem**
Genitive	**wessen**

Was remains unchanged in all cases and number.

Wer **mitgehen will, muß um fünf Uhr hier sein.**
Whoever wants to come along has to be here at 5:00.

You Need to Know ✔

Wer can only be used when there is no specific antecedent. References to specific people require regular relative pronouns (**der Mann, der . . . ; die Frau, die . . .**)

Was **auch immer passiert, ich habe keine Angst.**
Whatever happens, I am not afraid.

(The addition of **auch, immer, auch immer** intensifies the already indefinite character of these indefinite pronouns.)

The relative pronoun **was** (*that, which*) must be used if the antecedent is an indefinite pronoun such as **alles, nichts, etwas.**

Er erzählte mir etwas, *was* **ich schon wußte.**
He told me something that I knew already.

Was is also used when the antecedent is an entire clause.

Er hatte das Geld gewonnen, *was* **mich sehr freute.**
He had won the money, which made me very happy.

Wo is used as a relative pronoun when the antecedent is a place.

Er besuchte Berlin, *wo* **er viele Freunde hat.**
He visited Berlin, where he has many friends.

Wo-*compounds in relative clauses*

When relative pronouns are preceded by prepositions and refer to things or ideas (not people), they may be replaced with **wo-**compounds.

Das Paket, *worauf* (auf das) **er wartet, soll heute ankommen.**
The package for which he is waiting should arrive today.

Chapter 6
ADJECTIVES
AND ADVERBS

Demonstrative Adjectives

Demonstrative adjectives are used to point out or give special emphasis to the nouns they modify. In German the definite article **der, das, die** can also function as a demonstrative adjective, corresponding to the English *this* (plural, *these*) and *that* (plural, *those*). The demonstrative adjective, like the definite article, agrees with the noun it modifies in gender, number, and case. Thus the demonstrative

81

adjective has the same endings as the definite article. (*See* Chap. 3.)
When used as demonstrative adjectives, the various forms of **der, das,
die** are stressed in spoken German.

dieser, dieses, diese

Another demonstrative adjective is **dieser**. Like **der, das, die**, it agrees
with the noun it modifies in gender, number, and case and takes the
same endings as the definite article.

> *Diese* **Häuser sind sehr alt.**   *These houses are very old.*
> **Ich fahre mit** *diesem* **Bus.**   *I am taking this bus.*

Descriptive Adjectives

Descriptive adjectives are words that describe or provide additional
information about the qualities of people and things. In German, as in
English, descriptive adjectives can be used in various ways.

Predicate Adjective

When the adjective follows a noun or pronoun subject and is preceded
by a form of **sein, werden, bleiben**, it is a predicate adjective.

> **Der Kaffee war** *bitter.*   *The coffee was bitter.*
> **Seine Haare werden** *grau.*   *His hair is getting gray.*

The predicate adjective never takes an ending. Here are some common
German adjectives:

alt	*old*	**interessant**	*interesting*
amerikanisch	*American*	**jung**	*young*
arm	*poor*	**kalt**	*cold*
bequem	*comfortable*	**klein**	*small, short*
billig	*inexpensive*	**klug**	*clever, smart*
bitter	*bitter*	**krank**	*ill*
blond	*blond*	**kurz**	*short*

böse	*angry, mad*	**lang**	*long*
deutsch	*German*	**langsam**	*slow*
dick	*fat, thick*	**leer**	*empty*
dunkel	*dark*	**leicht**	*light, easy*
dünn	*thin, skinny*	**nah**	*near*
eng	*narrow*	**nett**	*nice*
faul	*lazy*	**neu**	*new*
fleißig	*industrious*	**reich**	*rich*
fremd	*strange*	**sauber**	*clean*
frisch	*fresh*	**sauer**	*sour*
gesund	*healthy*	**scharf**	*sharp, pungent*
glücklich	*happy*	**schmutzig**	*dirty*
groß	*big, tall*	**schnell**	*fast*
gut	*good*	**schwach**	*weak*
häßlich	*ugly*	**süß**	*sweet*
heiß	*hot*	**teuer**	*expensive*
hübsch	*pretty*	**voll**	*full*
intelligent	*intelligent*	**weit**	*far*

Attributive Adjective
Preceded by Definite Articles or other "der" Words

An adjective that precedes the noun is an attributive adjective, which in German always takes an ending. The adjective ending is determined by the number, gender, and the case of the noun it modifies. Another important factor determining the ending of the adjective is the presence or absence of a "**der**" or "**ein**" word.

The following words take the same endings as the definite article and are thus referred to as "**der**" words.

dieser	*this*	**solcher**	*such* (usually only plural)
jeder	*each, every* (only singular)	**welcher**	*which*
jener	*that*	**alle**	*all* (used only in plural)
mancher	*many (a)*		

When the attributive adjective modifies a noun and is preceded by the definite article or a "**der**" word, it takes the following endings.

	Singular			*Plural*
	Masculine	*Neuter*	*Feminine*	*All Genders*
Nominative	-e	-e	-e	-en
Accusative	-en	-e	-e	-en
Dative	-en	-en	-en	-en
Genitive	-en	-en	-en	-en

Nominative case, singular

Der alte **Tisch ist kaputt.**	*The old table is broken.*
Dieses kleine **Kind schreit.**	*This small child is screaming.*
Die nette **Frau hilft uns.**	*The nice woman is helping us.*

Note!

Two or more adjectives in succession all take the same endings.

Wo ist die *kleine, schwarze* **Katze?**
Where is the small, black cat?

Accusative case, singular

Ich kenne *den großen* **Mann.**	*I know the tall man.*
Sie läuft in *die alte* **Fabrik.**	*She is running into the old factory.*
Welche billige **Uhr hat er?**	*Which cheap watch does he have?*

Dative case, singular

Sie gibt *dem armen* **Mann Geld.**	*She gives the poor man money.*
Er wohnt bei *jener netten* **Familie.**	*He lives with that nice family.*
Trink aus *dem roten* **Glas!**	*Drink out of the red glass.*

Genitive case, singular

Dort ist die Mutter *des* *kleinen* **Kindes.**	*There is the mother of the small child.*
Er wohnt jenseits *dieses* *hohen* **Berges.**	*He lives on the other side of this high mountain.*

Plural, all cases, all genders

Diese frischen **Eier sind teuer.**	*These fresh eggs are expensive.*
Ich habe *alle leeren* **Flaschen.**	*I have all the empty bottles.*
Mit *solchen neuen* **Autos** **kann man schnell fahren.**	*One can drive fast with such new cars.*
Das Leben *jener alten* **Leute** **ist traurig.**	*The life of those old people is sad.*

Attributive Adjective
Preceded by Indefinite Articles or other "ein" Words

The negative article **kein** and all the possessives are called "**ein**" words, because they take the same endings as the indefinite article.

When the attributive adjective modifies a noun and is preceded by the indefinite article or an "**ein**" word, it takes the following endings.

	S i n g u l a r			*P l u r a l*
	Masculine	*Neuter*	*Feminine*	*All Genders*
Nominative	**-er**	**-es**	**-e**	**-en**
Accusative	**-en**	**-es**	**-e**	**-en**
Dative	**-en**	**-en**	**-en**	**-en**
Genitive	**-en**	**-en**	**-en**	**-en**

Nominative case, singular

Mein alter **Tisch ist kaputt.**	*My old table is broken.*
Ein kleines **Kind schreit.**	*A small child is screaming.*
Wo ist *deine nette* **Frau?**	*Where is your pleasant wife?*
Hier ist *unser altes* **Radio.**	*Here is our old radio.*

Accusative case, singular

Er liest *einen langen* **Roman.**	*He is reading a long novel.*
Habt ihr *kein scharfes* **Messer.**	*Don't you have a sharp knife.*
Ich suche *eine neue* **Wohnung.**	*I'm looking for a new apartment.*

Dative case, singular

Es gehört *ihrem reichen* **Onkel.**	*It belongs to her rich uncle.*
Er schläft auf *einem harten* **Bett.**	*He sleeps on a hard bed.*
Ich helfe *meiner alten* **Oma.**	*I'm helping my old granny.*

Genitive case, singular

Die Farbe *meines alten* **Wagens** **ist häßlich.**	*The color of my old car is ugly.*
Wann beginnt der Bau *eures neuen* **Hauses?**	*When does the construction of your new house begin?*
Trotz *ihrer wichtigen* **Arbeit macht sie Urlaub.**	*In spite of her important work she's taking a vacation.*

Plural, all cases, all genders

Seine alten **Freunde fliegen ab.**	*His old friends are departing.*
Wer hat *meine roten* **Bleistifte?**	*Who has my red pencils?*
Wir trinken aus *keinen schmutzigen* **Tassen.**	*We don't drink out of any dirty cups.*
Die Lehrerin *unserer kleinen* **Kinder ist hier.**	*The teacher of our small children is here.*

Attributive Adjective
Not Preceded by "der" or "ein" Words (Unpreceded Adjectives)

When the attributive adjective is not preceded by a "**der**" or "**ein**" word, the adjective requires an ending to indicate the number, gender, and case of the noun it modifies. The adjective endings coincide with the endings of the definite article except in the genitive singular, masculine and neuter.

When the attributive adjective modifies a noun and is unpreceded, it takes the following endings.

| | Singular | | | Plural |
	Masculine	Neuter	Feminine	All Genders
Nominative	-er	-es	-e	-e
Accusative	-en	-es	-e	-e
Dative	-em	-em	-er	-en
Genitive	-en	-en	-er	-er

Nominative case, singular

Alt<u>er</u> **Wein ist teuer.**	*Old wine is expensive.*
Das ist *deutsch<u>es</u>* **Geld.**	*That is German money.*
Frisch<u>e</u> **Luft ist gesund.**	*Fresh air is healthy.*

Note: With the absence of a "**der**" or "**ein**" word to provide grammatical information about the noun, here the adjective takes on this function by adding "**der**-word" endings to the adjective.

The nominative adjective endings are often used in forms of address.

Lieber **Onkel Franz!**	*Dear uncle Franz.*
Du *armes* **Kind!**	*You poor child!*

Accusative case, singular

Trinkt ihr *schwarzen* **Kaffee?**	*Do you drink black coffee?*
Sie ißt gern *weißes* **Brot.**	*She likes to eat white bread.*
Maria bestellte *kalte* **Milch.**	*Maria ordered cold milk.*

Salutations are in the accusative case.

Guten **Morgen!** *Guten* **Tag!**	*Good morning! Hello!*
Guten **Abend!** *Gute* **Nacht!**	*Good evening! Good night!*

Genitive case, singular

Trotz *starken* **Regens ging er spazieren.**	*He took a walk despite heavy rain.*
Schweren **Herzens reiste er ab.**	*He departed with a heavy heart.*
Sie war wegen *anstrengender* **Arbeit müde**	*She was tired because of taxing work.*

Plural, all cases, all genders

Alte **Perserteppiche sind teuer.**	*Old Persian rugs are expensive.*
Er hat *nette, brave* **Kinder.**	*He has nice, well-behaved children.*
Ich wohne bei *netten* **Leuten.**	*I live with nice people.*
Das Dorf liegt jenseits *hoher* **Berge.**	*The village lies on the other side of tall mountains.*

(*Note:* **hoch** drops the **c** when an adjective ending is added)

One of the following indefinite adjectives may precede the attributive adjective, in which case **both** take the plural unpreceded adjective endings. (These are the endings of the plural definite article.)

andere	*other*	**mehrere**	*several*
einige	*some, several*	**viele**	*many*
		wenige	*few*

Viele junge **Leute waren krank.**	*Many young people were ill.*
Wir sahen *mehrere wilde* **Hunde.**	*We saw several wild dogs.*
Das Leben *einiger alter* **Leute ist schwer.**	*The life of some old people is hard.*

Adjectival Constructions: Adjectives Derived from Verbs

Present Participles Used as Adjectives

In both English and German the present participle can be used as an attributive adjective. In English the present participle ends in *-ing*. In German it is formed by adding a **-d** to the infinitive: **lachend** (*laughing*), **singend** (*singing*). When used attributively, the appropriate adjective endings are added in German.

Das *weinende* **Kind tut mir leid.**	*I feel sorry for the crying child.*
Er ist in der *brennenden* **Fabrik.**	*He is in the burning factory.*
Wer ist der *regierende* **König?**	*Who is the reigning king?*

Past Participles Used as Adjectives

The past participles of both weak and strong verbs can be used as adjectives. (*See* Chap. 4 on the formation of past participles.) When used attributively, adjective endings are added to the past participles.

Gib mir das *gestohlene* **Geld!**   *Give me the stolen money.*
Sie ißt ein *weichgekochtes* **Ei.**   *She is eating a soft-boiled egg.*
Er ist am *geöffneten* **Fenster.**   *He is at the opened window.*

Adjectives Used as Nouns

In German many adjectives can also function as nouns. When used in this way, the adjective is capitalized and given a definite article that corresponds to natural gender. The endings of nouns created in this way follow the same patterns as the adjective endings described above.

der/die Kranke   *the sick person (masculine/feminine)*
ein Kranker/eine Kranke   *a sick person (masc./fem.)*
Kranke   *sick persons*

The use of adjectival nouns is much more widespread in German than it is in English. In German an adjectival noun can be used to refer to a specific individual or a group of individuals.

Ein *Toter* **lag auf der Straße.**   *A dead (man) lay in the street.*
Sie sieht den *Alten*.   *She sees the old one (man).*
Wer hilft den *Armen*?   *Who helps the poor?*

Adjectival nouns are also created from adjectives that have been derived from the present participle and the past participle of verbs. The endings taken by these adjectival nouns also are determined by whether they follow a **"der"** or an **"ein"** word or are unpreceded.

der/die Reisende	*traveler*
der/die Schreiende	*the screaming one*
der/die Verletzte	*injured/wounded person*
der/die Gefangene	*prisoner*
das Gehackte	*ground meat*

Adjectives following **etwas** (*something*), **nichts** (*nothing*), **viel** (*much*), **wenig** (*little*) are neuter and are capitalized

Er macht viel *Gutes.*	*He does much good.*
Ich habe nichts *Neues* **gehört.**	*I haven't heard anything new.*

Possessive Adjectives

Singular		*Plural*	
mein	*my*	**unser**	*our*
dein	*your (familiar)*	**euer**	*your*
sein	*his*		
sein	*its*		
ihr	*her*	**ihr**	*their*
Ihr	*your (formal)*	**Ihr**	*your (formal)*

Remember!

The possessive **Ihr** *(your,* singular and plural for formal address) is always capitalized.

The possessive adjectives are "**ein**" words and thus take the same set of endings as the indefinite article (*See* Chap. 3). These endings are determined by the gender, number, and case of the noun that the possessive adjective modifies. The choice of which possessive adjective to use in a given situation, however, is determined by who or what possesses the noun in question.

Wo ist *ihr* Bruder?   *Where is her brother?*

The ending of the possessive adjective **ihr** (*her*) is masculine, singular, nominative because the word **Bruder** is here masculine, singular, nominative. The choice of the third person, singular, feminine possessive **ihr** is determined by whose brother it is.

Ist das *seine* Mutter?   *Is that his mother?*

Here the ending on **seine** is feminine, singular, nominative corresponding to how the word **Mutter** is used.

Ich fahre *euren* Wagen.   *I drive your* (plural) *car.*

The possessive **euer** is normally contracted to **eur-** when an adjective ending is added.

Er sitzt in *unserem* Auto.   *He is sitting in our car.*
Ich nehme *meine* Kamera.   *I take my camera.*
Die Farbe *seines* Autos ist rot.   *The color of his car is red.*

Comparison of Adjectives and Adverbs

In German adjectives have three degrees of comparison:

Positive	**klein**	*small, short*
Comparative	**kleiner**	*smaller, shorter*
Superlative	**kleinst-**	
	am kleinsten	*smallest, shortest the smallest*

The comparative of an adjective is formed by adding **-er** to the base form of the adjective. Many common one-syllable adjectives take an umlaut in the comparative and superlative. Note table below.

Helga ist *kleiner* als Gisela.   *Helga is shorter than Gisela.*
Hans ist *älter* als Jörg.   *Hans is older than Jörg.*

The superlative is formed by adding **-st** to the adjective. Note that

-est is added to adjectives ending in **-d, -t, -s, -ß, -st, -x, -z, -sch**. The superlative form always requires an ending. The superlative form **am** _____ **(e)sten** is used with a predicative adjective.

Anna ist das _kleinste_ **Mädchen.**	_Anna is the shortest girl._
Anna ist _am kleinsten._	_Anna is the shortest._

Unlike in English, it is **not** possible in German to create compound comparative or superlative forms by adding such words as _more_ or _most_ to an adjective or adverb. Compare the forms below.

modern	_modern_	
moderner	_more modern_	
am modernsten	_most modern_	

In English the suffix _-ly_ is usually added to an adjective to make it an adverb. In German no endings are added to the base form of the adjective. The comparative and superlative of the adverb is formed by adding **-er** and **am** _____ **-(e)sten** respectively to the adverb.

Hans fährt _schnell._	_Hans drives fast._
Inge fährt _schneller._	_Inge drives faster._
Kurt fährt _am schnellsten._	_Kurt drives fastest (of all)._

Maria singt _schön._	_Maria sings beautifully._
Ingo singt _schöner._	_Ingo sings more beautifully._
Sofie singt _am schönsten._	_Sofie sings most beautifully._

Vowel Change in Monosyllabic Adjectives

The stem vowels of the following monosyllabic adjectives add an umlaut in the comparatives and superlatives. Remember only **a, o,** and **u** take an umlaut in German.

Adjective/Adverb		Comparative	Superlative	
alt	*old*	älter	ältest-	am ältesten
arm	*poor*	ärmer	ärmst-	am ärmsten
hart	*hard*	härter	härtest-	am härtesten
jung	*young*	jünger	jüngst-	am jüngsten
kalt	*cold*	kälter	kältest-	am kältesten
klug	*smart*	klüger	klügst-	am klügsten
krank	*sick*	kränker	kränkst-	am kränksten
kurz	*short*	kürzer	kürzest-	am kürzesten
lang	*long*	länger	längst-	am längsten
oft	*often*	öfter	öftest-	am öftesten
scharf	*sharp*	schärfer	schärfst-	am schärfsten
schwach	*weak*	schwächer	schwächst-	am schwächsten
stark	*strong*	stärker	stärkst-	am stärksten
warm	*warm*	wärmer	wärmst-	am wärmsten

Irregular Adjectives and Adverbs

The adjective **hoch** drops the **c** in the comparative.

hoch	*high*	höher	höchst-	am höchsten

The adjective **nah** adds the **c** in the superlative.

nah	*near*	näher	nächst-	am nächsten

Other irregular adjectives and adverbs are as follows.

gern	*(to) like (to)*	lieber	liebst-	am liebsten
groß	*big, tall*	größer	größt-	am größten
gut	*good*	besser	best-	am besten
viel	*much*	mehr	meist-	am meisten

Comparisons

Comparison of inequality

Comparisons implying inequality are expressed with the comparative followed by **als** (*than*).

Erich ist *größer* **als ich.**	*Erich is taller than I.*
Der Ring ist *teurer* **als die Kette.**	*The ring is more expensive than the necklace.*

Immer *plus comparative form*

Immer plus the comparative form expresses an increase in degree.

Es wird *immer kälter.*	*It is getting colder and colder.*
Sie werden *immer reicher.*	*They are getting richer and richer.*

The superlative

The superlative form **am** _____ **-(e)sten** is always used as the superlative of adverbs. It is also used with predicate adjectives.

Dieses Auto ist *am teuersten.*	*This car is the most expensive.*
Ich laufe *am schnellsten.*	*I run the fastest.*
Inge springt *am höchsten.*	*Inge jumps the highest.*

Comparison of equality

Comparisons implying equality are expressed by **so . . . wie** *(as . . . as)*

Karl ist *so groß wie* **Gert.**	*Karl ist as tall as Gert.*
Sie fährt *so schnell wie* **ich.**	*She drives as fast as I do.*
Peter ist *so stark wie* **Max.**	*Peter is as strong as Max.*

Comparative and superlative forms as attributive adjectives

The comparative and superlative forms of adjectives take the same endings as the positive or base forms of the adjectives.

Das ist der billiger*e* **Mantel.**	*That is the cheaper coat.*
Er liest den längst*en* **Roman.**	*He is reading the longest novel.*
Das ist ein größer*er* **Wagen.**	*That is a larger car.*
Er hilft einem älter*en* **Mann.**	*He is helping an older man.*

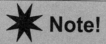

Note!

The comparative forms of **mehr** and **weniger** do not add adjective endings in the singular or plural.

Sie hat *mehr* **Bücher als du.**   *She has more books than you.*
Hast du *weniger* **Geld?**   *Do you have less money?*

Adverbs

The adverb **sehr** (*very*) precedes an adjective or adverb to express a high degree of a certain quality.

Dieses Auto fährt *sehr* **schnell.**	*This car goes very fast.*
Sie ist *sehr* **intelligent.**	*She is very intelligent.*
Im Sommer ist es *sehr* **heiß.**	*It is very hot in summer.*

Many German adverbs do not have a corresponding adjective form. Such adverbs can refer to time, manner, or place. Here are a few.

Adverbs Referring to Time

abends	*in the evenings*	**morgens**	*in the mornings*
bald	*soon*	**nachts**	*at night*
damals	*at that time*	**nie**	*never*
gestern	*yesterday*	**nun**	*now*
heute	*today*	**oft**	*often*
immer	*always*	**selten**	*seldom, rarely*
jetzt	*now*	**spät**	*late*
manchmal	*at times, sometimes*	**täglich**	*daily, every day*

Adverbs Referring to Manner

gern	*gladly*	**sicherlich**	*certainly*
hoffentlich	*hopefully*	**so**	*so*
leider	*unfortunately*	**vielleicht**	*perhaps, maybe*
natürlich	*naturally*	**wirklich**	*really*

nicht	not	ziemlich	rather
schon	already	zu	to

Adverbs Referring to Place

da	there	links	(on, to the) left
dort	there	oben	above, upstairs
draußen	outside	rechts	(on, to the) right
drinnen	inside	überall	everywhere
hier	here	weg	away
hinten	in the back		

Position of Adverbs

In German the adverb usually follows the verb and pronoun. If more than one adverb occurs in a series, the following order is observed: time, manner, place (Use the word "TEMPO" to remember this order of adverbial elements). **Nicht** precedes an adverb of place.

Er fährt _morgen_ _mit dem Bus_ _in die Stadt._ He is going by bus into
     (time) _(manner)_ _(place)_   town tomorrow.
Sie ist _jetzt leider draußen._   Unfortunately, she is outside now.
Er ist _heute wirklich nicht hier._   He is really not here today.

Idiomatic Use of Adverbs

German makes frequent use of a number of adverbs such as **denn, doch, ja** to convery the attitude or feelings of the speaker toward a situation or event. Sometimes called _flavoring particles_ and _intensifiers_, these adverbs are used in German to indicate surprise, emphasis, certainty, uncertainty, doubt, etc. which in English we would express through voice clues such as emphasis and intonation. Thus, there are no directly equivalent translations for these adverbs.

denn
    Denn expresses impatience, curiosity, or interest in questions.

    Wo ist er _denn?_   _Well, where is he?_

doch

Doch occurs both stressed and unstressed. When stressed, it expresses that something happened despite expectations to the contrary. It is also used instead of **ja** (*yes*) as an answer to a negative question.

Ich habe es *doch* **verkauft.**	*I sold it after all.*
Trinkst du nichts? *Doch,*	*Aren't you drinking anything? Yes*
ich trinke Tee.	*(sure), I'm drinking tea.*

When **doch** is unstressed, it expresses that the opposite is not expected to be true. In an imperative construction, **doch** corresponds to English *"why don't you ..."* **Doch** can also be used for emphasis.

Sie ist *doch* **nicht in Köln!**	*She isn't in Cologne, is she?*
Kauf ihm *doch* **etwas!**	*Why don't you buy him something?*

ja

This adverb reinforces an idea, observation, or fact.

Sie ist *ja* **verrückt.**	*Why, she is crazy.*
Ich war *ja* **krank.**	*After all, I was ill.*

Chapter 7

NUMBERS, DATES, TIME

IN THIS CHAPTER:

✔ *Cardinal Numbers*
✔ *Measurements, Prices, and other Decimal Fractions*
✔ *Ordinal Numbers*
✔ *Fractions*
✔ *Dates*
✔ *Time*

Cardinal Numbers

The cardinal numbers in German are as follows.

0	null	6	sechs
1	eins	7	sieben
2	zwei	8	acht
3	drei	9	neun
4	vier	10	zehn
5	fünf	11	elf

12	zwölf	100	hundert
13	dreizehn	101	hunderteins
14	vierzehn	120	hundertzwanzig
15	fünfzehn	123	hundertdreiundzwanzig
16	sechzehn	200	zweihundert
17	siebzehn	300	dreihundert
18	achtzehn	999	neunhundertneunund-
19	neunzehn		neunzig
20	zwanzig	1 000	tausend
21	einundzwanzig	1 001	tausendeins
22	zweiundzwanzig	1 110	tausendeinhun-
30	dreißig		dertzehn
35	fünfunddreißig	1 999	tausendneunhun-
40	vierzig		dertneunundneunzig
70	siebzig	*in dates:*	neunzehnhundert-
90	neunzig		neunundneunzig

Note that for large numbers German uses a space or a period where English would use a comma (**tausendeins:** 1 001 **or** 1.001). **Eine Million, eine Milliarde** *(1 000 000 000)*, and **eine Billion** *(1 000 000 000 000)* are nouns, thus capitalized and have plural forms.

Measurements, Prices, and Other Decimal Fractions

Decimal fractions for prices and various measurements, normally expressed with a decimal point or period in English, are represented in German by a comma.

	German	*English*
2,3	**zwei komma drei**	2.3
4,45	**vier komma fünfundvierzig**	4.45
1,00 DM	**eine Mark**	DM 1.00
6,01 DM	**sechs Mark eins**	DM 6.01

Ordinal Numbers

Ordinal numbers *up to nineteenth* are formed by adding **-t** to the cardinal numbers. Ordinals from *twentieth to hundreth* add **-st**. Since ordinal numbers are adjectives in German they also require adjective endings.

Note the irregular forms for *first and third*.

1. der, die, das erste	25. der, die, das fünfundzwanzigste	
2. der, die, das zweite	100. der, die, das hundertste	
3. der, die, das dritte	101. der, die, das hunderterste	
7. der, die, das siebte	1000. der, die, das tausendste	

In German a period following a number indicates that it is an ordinal:

Wilhelm I. (Wilhelm der Erste) *Wilhelm the first*
Heute haben wir **den 2. Mai (den zweiten Mai-***accusative***).**
Today is the second of May
Sie wohnt **im 3. Stock (im dritten Stock** -*dative***).**
She lives on the third floor.

Fractions

Fractions can be used as neuter nouns or as adjectives and are formed by adding **-el** to the ordinal numbers. No adjective endings are required for fractions: 1/3 = **ein drittel (das Drittel)**, 1/5 = **ein fünftel (das Fünftel)**, 3/4 = **drei viertel (drei Viertel)**, 5/6 - **fünf sechstel.**

Important!

The fraction 1/2 has two forms: **die (eine) Hälfte** (noun) or **halb** (adj.). The adjectival form **halb** requires adjective endings. There are also special forms for 1 1/2: **eineinhalb; anderthalb; ein und ein halb.**

Dates

Days of the week

der Montag	*Monday*	**der Freitag**	*Friday*
der Dienstag	*Tuesday*	**der Samstag** *or*	
der Mittwoch	*Wednesday*	**der Sonnabend**	*Saturday*
der Donnerstag	*Thursday*	**der Sonntag**	*Sunday*

The contraction **am** (**an dem**) is used with the names of the days (**am Montag** = *on Monday*). Note that all days of the week and months are masculine.

Months

der Januar	*January*	**der Juli**	*July*
der Februar	*February*	**der August**	*August*
der März	*March*	**der September**	*September*
der April	*April*	**der Oktober**	*October*
der Mai	*May*	**der November**	*November*
der Juni	*June*	**der Dezember**	*December*

Seasons

The seasons as well are all masculine: **der Frühlling** (*spring*), **der Sommer** (*summer*), **der Herbst** (*fall*), **der Winter** (*winter*).

In German time expressions, the contraction **im** (**in dem**) precedes the name of the month or season, **im Herbst** (in the fall). The preposition **in** however does not precede the year unless the expression **im Jahre** is used:

> **Der Krieg war *1918* vorbei.** *The war was over in 1918.*
> **Er schrieb es *im Jahre* 1935.** *He wrote it in (the year)1935.*

Time

To ask for the time of day German uses the following:

> **Wieviel Uhr ist es?** or **Wie spät ist es?** (*What time is it?*)

The answer will be: (1:00) **Es ist ein Uhr (Es ist eins)**; (3:05) **Es ist ist fünf (Minuten) nach drei**; (4:15) **Es ist (ein) Viertel nach vier**; (4:30) **Es ist halbfünf**; (4:45) **Es ist Viertel vor fünf.**

The idiom **um . . . Uhr** corresponds to *at . . . o'clock:*

Der Zug kommt um zwei Uhr (nachts, nachmittags) an.
Sie kommt um sechs Uhr (morgens, abends).

Note that in colloquial speech, adverbs of time are used to clarify a.m. and p.m. when necessary. However, **official time** in Germany (at airports, railroad stations, in the public media) is based on the 24 hour system: **vierundzwanzig Uhr** = *Midnight;* **dreizehn Uhr** = *1:00 p.m.*

Periods of the Day

The periods of the day are preceded by the contraction **am:**

am Morgen	*in the morning*	**am Abend**	*in the evening*
am Mittag	*at noon*		
am Nachmittag	*in the afternoon*	But: ***In der* Nacht**	*at night*

Ich gehe *am Abend* **spazieren.**   *I take a walk in the evening.*
Wo bist du *in der* **Nacht?**   *Where are you at night?*

Other Adverbs of Time

heute	*today*	**vorgestern**	*the day before yesterday*
morgen	*tomorrow*		
übermorgen	*the day after tomorrow*	**heute morgen**	*this morning*
		gestern abend	*last night*
gestern	*yesterday*	**morgen nachmittag**	*tomorrow afternoon*

Wir haben *gestern nachmittag* **Tennis**   We played tennis
    gespielt.   yesterday afternoon.

Time Expressions in the Accusative and Genitive Cases

Time expressions referring to a **definite time** or a **duration of time** require the **accusative** case. Expressions of **indefinite time** require the **genitive** case in German.

Ich gehe *jeden Tag* **zur Arbeit.**	*I go to work every day.*
Letzten Sommer **war ich in Ulm.**	*I was in Ulm last summer.*
Wir bleiben *ein ganzes Jahr.*	*We'll stay one entire year.*
Eines Tages **besuchte ich sie.**	*One day I visited her.*
Ich zeige es dir *eines Tages.*	*I'll show it to you someday.*
Eines Abends **kam er nicht.**	*One evening he didn't come.*

Time Expressions in the Dative Case

Time expressions using the prepositions **an, in, vor** require the dative case. *Ago* is expressed by the preposition **vor** which precedes the time expression.

Wir gehen *am Morgen.*	*We are going in the morning.*
Im Sommer *segeln wir.*	*We go sailing in the summer.*
Er hat **im Dezember** *Geburtstag.*	*His birthday is in December.*
Er war **vor einer Woche** *in Afrika.*	*A week ago he was in Africa.*
Sie war **vor acht Tagen** *hier.*	*She was here eight days ago.*

You Need to Know

- Times of the day
- Months and seasons of the year
- Cardinal and ordinal numbers

Chapter 8

PREPOSITIONS

Prepositions and their Cases

Prepositions are words that in combination with a noun or pronoun show position, direction, time, or manner (such as *under* the table, *to* the store, *in* April, *without* a word).

In English the noun or pronoun following a preposition is always in the same case (e.g., with *him*, behind *him*, for *him*, by *him*). In German, however, prepositions can be followed by the accusative, dative, or genitive case. Consequently, when learning the prepositions in German, it is necessary to memorize which case each particular preposition requires.

It is also important to bear in mind that the use of prepositions within a language is hightly idiomatic, and thus prepositional usage in German does not necessarily correspond to English usage.

Prepositions Governing the Accusative Case

The following prepositions always require the accusative case.

bis—*by, until, up to* (*Note:* **bis** can be used alone or in combination with another preposition. When used alone, it is followed by the accusative case; when **bis** is followed by another preposition, the second preposition determines the case that follows.)

> **Er bleibt** *bis* **nächsten Montag.** *He'll stay* until *next Monday.*
> **Ich laufe** *bis zur* **Ecke.** *I'll walk* up to *the corner.*

durch—*through, by*

> **Er läuft** *durch* **das Zimmer.** *He is running* through *the room.*
> **Er wurde** *durch* **einen Schuß getötet.** *He was killed by a shot.*

entlang—*along* (*Note:* **entlang** *follows* the accusative object; when it precedes its object, it takes the dative.)

> **Wir gehen die Straße** *entlang.* *We are walking* along *the street.*

für—*for*

> **Er kaufte es** *für* **seinen Freund.** *He bought it* for *his friend.*
> **Sie arbeitet** *für* **meine Eltern.** *She works* for *my parents.*

gegen—*against, toward, about*

> **Ich bin** *gegen* **den Krieg.** *I am* against *the war.*
> **Er kämpfte** *gegen* **den Meister.** *He fought* against *the champion.*

ohne—*without*

> *Ohne* **seine Frau kommt er nie.** *He never comes* without *his wife.*
> **Er geht nicht** *ohne* **sein Kind.** *He won't go* without *his child.*

Important Point!

The prepositions **durch, für, um** often contract with **das** to form **durchs, fürs, ums,** unless the article functions as a demonstrative or the noun is followed by a descriptive clause.

um—*around*
> **Hans fährt *um* das Haus.**   *Hans drives* around *the house.*
> **Die Familie sitzt *um* den Tisch.**   *The family sits* around *the table.*

Prepositions Governing the Dative Case

The following prepositions are always followed by the dative case.

aus—*out of, from* (point of origin; denotes coming from place of birth or domicile), *of* (usually without an article)

> **Helga kommt *aus* dem Hotel.**   *Helga is coming* out of *the hotel.*
> **Kommen Sie *aus* Deutschland?**   *Do you come* from *Germany?*
> **Das Messer ist *aus* Stahl.**   *The knife is (made)* of *steel.*

außer—*except (for), besides*
> *Außer* **dem Chef waren alle da.**   Except for *the boss all were here.*
> *Außer* **diesem Volkswagen**   *I own nothing* besides *this*
>   **besitze ich nichts.**   *Volkswagen.*

bei—*with* (at the home of), *near, at*
> **Ich wohne *bei* meinem Onkel.**   *I am living* with *my uncle.*
> **Wohnst du *bei* der Schule?**   *Do you live* near *the school?*
> **Ich treffe dich *bei* der Uni.**   *I'll meet you* at *the university.*

gegenüber—*across (from)* (usually follows the dative object)
> **Er wohnt dem Park *gegenüber.***   *He lives* across from *the park.*
> **Sie sitzt ihren Eltern *gegenüber.***   *She sits* across from *her parents.*

mit—*with, by (means of)*
> **Ich reise *mit* diesen Leuten.**   *I am traveling* with *these people.*
> **Sie fährt *mit* dem Zug.**   *She is going* by *train.*

nach—*after, according to* (with this meaning, **nach** usually *follows* the noun), *to* (no article with neuter geographical names)

> *Nach* **dem Essen gehen wir aus.**   *We'll go out* after *the meal.*
> **Ihm *nach* war es falsch.**   *According to him it was wrong.*
> **Sie flog *nach* Deutschland.**   *She flew* to *Germany.*

seit—*since, for* (with time expressions)

Seit **seiner Kindheit wohnt er in Ulm.**	*He has been living in Ulm* since *his childhood.*
Ich kenne ihn *seit* **einem Jahr.**	*I have known him* for *one year.*

von—*from, by, of*

Die Uhr ist *von* **meiner Mutter.**	*The watch is* from *my mother.*
Ist das ein Drama *von* **Goethe?**	*Is that a drama* by *Goethe?*

from (coming from a certain direction, as opposed to origin)

Der Zug kommt *von* **Ulm.**	*The train is coming* from Ulm.

by (used in passive constructions to express the agent, see Chap. 14)

Das Buch wurde *von* **Goethe geschrieben.**	*The book was written* by *Goethe.*

zu—*to* (direction toward people and places when no geographical name is used)

Wir gehen *zu* **dem Zahnarzt.**	*We're going* to *the dentist.*
Sie geht *zu* **der Buchmesse.**	*She is going* to *the book fair.*

Note!

The prepositions **bei, von, zu** contract with **dem** and **der** to form **beim, vom, zum, zur,** unless these articles function as demonstratives or the noun is followed by a descriptive clause.

Prepositions Governing the Accusative <u>or</u> Dative Case

Another group of German prepositions can be used with either the accusative or the dative. The case is determined by how they are used within the sentence.

The accusative case is used when the verb in combination with the preposition expresses *movement toward a place*. These prepositions answer the question "**wohin?**" ("where to"?). (*See* Chap. 9.)

The dative case is used when the verb in combination with the preposition expresses *position, location*. These prepositions answer the question "**wo?**" ("where?" or "in what place?"). (*See* Chap. 9.)

Accusative	**Dative**
an—*to, onto*	*at*
Der Hund läuft *an die* **Tür**	**Der Hund steht** *an der* **Tür.**
The dog runs to *the door.*	*The dog stands* at *the door.*
auf—*on, on top of, onto, upon*	on
Er legt das Messer *auf den* **Tisch**	**Das Messer liegt** *auf dem* **Tisch.**
He lays the knife on *the table.*	*The knife is lying* on *the table.*
hinter—*behind*	*behind*
Erich geht *hinter das* **Haus**	**Erich spielt** *hinter dem* **Haus.**
Erich goes behind *the house.*	*Erich plays* behind *the house.*
in—*in, into, to*	*in*
Die Kinder gehen *in die* **Schule.**	**Die Kinder sind** *in der* **Schule**
The children go to *school.*	*The children are* in *school.*
neben—*beside, next to*	*beside, next to*
Setze dich *neben diesen* **Herrn.**	**Ich sitze** *neben diesem* **Herrn.**
Sit down beside *this gentleman.*	*I sit* beside *this gentleman.*
über—*over, above, across*	*over, above, across*
Hänge das Bild *über den* **Tisch.**	**Das Bild hängt** *über dem* **Tisch.**
Hang the picture over *the table.*	*The picture hangs* over *the table.*

unter—*under, below, among*   *under, below, beneath*

Der Ball rollte *unter den* **Stuhl.**   **Der Ball ist** *unter dem* **Stuhl.**
The ball rolled under *the chair.*   *The ball is* under *the chair.*

vor—*in front of, before*   *in front of, before*

Er setzt sich *vor den* **Fernseher.**   **Er sitzt** *vor dem* **Fernseher.**
He sits down in front of *the TV.*   *He sits* in front of *the TV.*

zwischen—*between*   *between*

Sie hat den Brief *zwischen das*   **Der Brief liegt jetzt** *zwischen*
Buch und *die* **Zeitung gelegt.**   *dem* **Buch und** *der* **Zeitung.**
She placed the letter between *the*   *The letter is now lying* between
book and the newspaper.   *the book and the newspaper.*

Remember!

The prepositions **an, auf, in, hinter, über, unter, vor** usually contract with the accusative **das** and the dative **dem** to form **ans, am, aufs, ins, im, hinters, übers, unters, vors** unless the articles function as demonstratives or the noun is followed by a descriptive clause.

There are, however, many idiomatic constructions using these *either-or* prepositions where the movement/lack of movement distinction is not applicable. In such instances the cases following the prepositions must be learned. Here are just a few examples.

Verb phrases with **auf, über** are often followed by the *accusative*.

lachen über	*to laugh about*	**Wir lachten über** *den Clown.*
sprechen über	*to speak about*	**Sprecht ihr über** *die alte Frau?*
warten auf	*to wait for*	**Sie wartet auf** *den letzten Zug.*

An, in, unter, vor, zwischen often take the dative case

erkennen an	*to recognize*	**Man erkennt ihn an** *dem Bart.*
Angst haben vor	*to be afraid of*	**Er hat Angst vor** *dem Hund.*

Da- and Wo- Compounds

Da- Compounds with Prepositions

Da- compounds are used when referring to inanimate objects or abstract ideas discussed in a previous sentence. They are used the same way as the English pronouns *it* and *them* with prepositions. In German the **da-** form is used regardless of the gender or number of the noun it replaces. If the preposition starts with a vowel, **dar-** is prefixed (**darin, darauf, darüber**). Note that these **da(r)**-compounds are *never used to refer to people.* (*See* Chap. 5.)

Bist du *gegen den Plan?*	*Are you against the plan?*
Ja, ich bin *dagegen.*	*Yes, I am against it.*
Denkst du *an die Ferien?*	*Are you thinking about vacation?*
Nein, ich denke nicht *daran.*	*No, I am not thinking about it.*
Was macht er *mit dem Kuli?*	*What is he doing with the pen?*
Er schreibt *damit.*	*He is writing with it.*

All accusative, dative, and accusative/dative prepositions can be prefixed by **da(r)-** except for **entlang, ohne, außer, seit.**

Wo- Compounds with Prepositions

In German the interrogative **was** (referring to things) is usually avoided after an accusative or dative preposition. Instead, **wo-** or **wor-** is prefixed to the preposition. The same guidelines and exceptions apply here as to the **da-** compounds above.

Womit **kann ich helfen?**	*What can I help you with?*
Worüber **sprecht ihr?**	*What are you talking about?*

Worauf **wartest du?**   *What are you waiting for?*

Prepositions Governing the Genitive Case

The most commonly occurring genitive prepositions are:

(an)statt—*instead of*
 (An)statt **seiner Schwester ist** *His aunt came* instead of
  seine Tante gekommen. *his sister.*

trotz—*in spite of, despite*
 Er kam *trotz* **seiner Krankheit.** *He came* in spite of *his illness.*

während—*during*
 Während **unserer Ferien** *We are going to Spain* during
  fahren wir nach Spanien. *our vacation.*

wegen—*because of*
 Wir konnten *wegen* **ihrer** *We could not depart* because of
  Verspätung nicht abfahren. *her delay.*

You Need to Know ✔

Other useful genitive prepositions include:

außerhalb—*outside of* **diesseits**—*on this side of*
innerhalb—*inside of, within* **jenseits**—*on the other side of*

oberhalb—*on the upper side, above* **um . . . willen**—*for the sake of*

unterhalb—*on the lower side, below*

Chapter 9
INTERROGATIVES AND NEGATIVES

IN THIS CHAPTER:

✔ *General Questions*
✔ *Specific Questions*
✔ *Negation*

General Questions

General questions are questions that can be answered by **ja** (*yes*) or **nein** (*no*). This type of question is formed by simply *inverting the subject and the verb* of the declarative sentence so that the verb is in first position (*See* Chap. 12). No interrogative word or phrase is used in forming this type of question. Any subject-verb combination may be inverted to form a general question. Compare the following patterns:

Statement = Subject + Verb (+ Remainder of Sentence).

S	+	V	(+ *remainder of sentence*).
Das Kind		**kommt**	(nach Hause).

General Question = Verb + Subject (+ Remainder of Sentence)?

V	+	*S*	(+ *remainder of sentence)?*
Kommt		**das Kind**	**(nach Hause)?**

In English a general question usually requires the use of an auxiliary verb (such as *to do, to be,* e.g. *Does she sing? Is he going too?),* whereas in German in the simple tenses the main verb is used by itself to introduce such questions **(Singt sie? Kommt er auch?).** In the compound tenses in German, however, it is the auxiliary verb (i.e., the conjugated verb) that is inverted and put in first position to introduce a general question.

Important!

Simple Tenses

Statement	*Question*
Robert reparierte das Auto.	*Reparierte* **Robert das Auto?**
Horst, du bist krank.	**Horst,** *bist* **du krank?**

Compound Tenses

Statement	*Question*
Du hast es gesehen.	*Hast* **du es** *gesehen?*
Du kannst es machen	*Kannst* **du es** *machen?*

Specific Questions

Specific questions are questions that ask for specific information. In both English and German this type of question is introduced by an interrogative word or phrase that seeks information about time, manner, place, or cause (as well as who or what may be the actor or recipient of some action). Here are some common interrogative adverbs:

Wann?	*When?*	**Wie oft?**	*How often?*
Warum?	*Why?*	**Wieviel?**	*How much, many?*
Wie?	*How?*	**Wie viele?**	*How many?*
Wie lange?	*How long?*	**Um wieviel Uhr?**	*At what time?*

Wann **kommt der Zug an?** *When is the train arriving?*
Warum **hast du nichts gesagt?** *Why didn't you say anything?*
Wieviel **kostet es?** *How much does it cost?*
Um wieviel Uhr **kommst du?** *At what time are you coming?*

In this case the verb is not in first position in the sentence, but is in second position following the interrogative adverb.

Wieviel or wie viele

Wieviel (*how much*) is used in specific questions and before singular nouns; **wie viele** (*how many*) is used before plural nouns.

Wieviel **kostet das?** *How much does it cost?*
Wieviel **Zeit hast du?** *How much time do you have?*

Wie viele **Kinder sind hier?** *How many children are here?*
Wie viele **Äpfel hast du gegessen?** *How many apples did you eat?*

Wo, wohin, woher

In German there are three different interrogatives to ask about place: **wo, wohin, woher.** Each word has its own distinct meaning.

The interrogative **wo** asks about *location* (*in what place?*). Normally **wo** is used when there is no destination or direction. The answer usually contains a preposition followed by the dative case.

Wo **seid ihr?**	**Wir sind in der Schule.**
Wo **wandert er?**	**Er wandert im Wald.**
Wo **ist das Buch?**	**Es liegt auf dem Tisch.**

The interrogative **wohin** asks about *destination* or *direction* (*to what place?*). The answer usually contains a preposition followed by the accusative case.

Wohin **geht ihr?**	**Wir gehen ins Theater.**
Wohin **fährst du heute?**	**Ich fahre heute in die Stadt.**

The interrogative **woher** asks about *origin* (*from what place?*).

Woher **kommst du?**	**Ich komme aus dem Wald.**
Woher **kommst Willi?**	**Er kommt aus Deutschland.**

Interrogative Adjective

Was für ein- (*what kind of*) is usually used as an interrogative adjective. In the singular, **ein-** takes adjective endings, determined by the way the noun that follows is used grammatically in the sentence. **Für** does not act as a preposition in these expressions. In the plural the expression is **was für.**

Was für eine **Maschine ist das?**	**Eine Drehmaschine.**
Mit was für einem **Herrn sprichst du?**	**Mit einem alten Herrn.**
Was für **Leute sind das?**	**Das sind Touristen.**

Negation

In German, the negation of verbs is most commonly expressed by the negative adverb **nicht**. The word **nicht** can be used to negate an entire sentence or individual units within a sentence.

Nicht in Final Position

Nicht always *follows:*

The inflected form of the verb (the form with the personal ending)

Sie liest.
Anton fragte.

Sie liest *nicht.*
Anton fragte *nicht.*

Noun objects (direct or indirect objects)

Wir besuchten die Dame.
Sie gab es dem Kind.
Er gab dem Mann den Tee.

Wir besuchten die Dame *nicht.*
Sie gab es dem Kind *nicht.*
Er gab dem Mann den Tee *nicht.*

Pronoun objects (direct or indirect object)

Gisela holte es.
Wir freuten uns.
Ich erklärte es ihr.

Gisela holte es *nicht.*
Wir freuten uns *nicht.*
Ich erklärte es ihr *nicht.*

Adverbs of definite time

Er besuchte uns gestern.   **Er besuchte uns gestern** *nicht.*

Nicht Preceding Other Elements in the Sentence

Nicht *precedes* most other elements:

Predicate adjectives and nouns

Er ist krank.
Das sind meine Kinder.

Er ist *nicht* **krank.**
Das sind *nicht* **meine Kinder.**

Separable prefixes

Das Flugzeug flog ab.	**Das Flugzeug flog** *nicht* **ab.**
Ilse steigt jetzt um.	**Ilse steigt jetzt** *nicht* **um.**

Past Participles

Sie sind gefahren.	**Sie sind** *nicht* **gefahren.**

Dependent infinitives

Wir hören sie lachen.	**Wir hören sie** *nicht* **lachen.**
Ich hoffe, es zu sehen.	**Ich hoffe, es** *nicht* **zu sehen.**

Adverbs of place or prepositional phrases

Mitzi wohnte hier.	**Mitzi wohnte** *nicht* **hier.**
Ich freue mich darauf.	**Ich freue mich** *nicht* **darauf.**
Wir sind im Wohnzimmer.	**Wir sind** *nicht* **im Wohnzimmer.**

When a past participle and a prepositional phrase or adverb of place occur in the same sentence, **nicht** precedes the prepositional phrase or adverb of place.

Ich habe im Sand gelegen.	**Ich habe** *nicht* **im Sand gelegen.**
Sie hat dort gespielt.	**Sie hat** *nicht* **dort gepielt.**

Other Negative Words

The negative words gar nicht (*not at all*), nicht mehr (*no more, no longer, anymore*), nie (*never*), noch nicht (*not yet*), and noch nie (*not ever, never*) follow the same rules for position that apply to nicht.

Negative Article kein-

Kein is used to negate nouns. **Kein-** (*no, not any, not a*) precedes a noun object or a predicate noun. It is used when the noun in the affirmative statement has an indefinite article or no article. **Kein** takes the same endings as the indefinite article. (See Chapter 5.)

Er hat einen Bruder.	**Er hat** *keinen* **Bruder.**
Wir trinken Milch.	**Wir trinken** *keine* **Milch.**

When the noun in the affirmative is preceded by a definite article, a "**der**" word, or a possessive adjective, **nicht** is used instead.

Dieses Bier schmeckt gut.	**Dieses Bier schmeckt** *nicht* **gut.**
Meine Tochter ist hier.	**Meine Tochter ist** *nicht* **hier.**
Der Hund bellt.	**Der Hund bellt** *nicht*.

Pronouns nichts, niemand

Nichts (*nothing*) and **niemand** (*nobody*) are used only in the singular. They require no endings. **Nichts** can be followed by a neuter adjective used as a noun.

Er hat *nichts* **gekauft.**	*He bought nothing.*
Er hat *nichts Neues* **gekauft.**	*He bought nothing new.*
Ich kenne *niemand*.	*I know nobody.*

Chapter 10
VOCABULARY

This chapter provides the student of German with some selected basic vocabulary items useful for everyday situations.

At the airport
Am Flughafen

abfahren	to leave (trains, buses)
abfliegen	to leave (airplanes)
der Abflug	departure
abholen	to pick up
ankommen	to arrive
die Ankunft	arrival
aufrufen, durchsagen	to announce
der Ausgang	gate
der Auslandsflug	international flight
der Bahnhof	railroad station
bereit	ready
der Bus	bus
das Fenster	window
fliegen	to fly
der Flug	flight
die Fluggesellschaft (die Fluglinie)	airline
der Flughafen	airport
das Flugzeug	airplane
frei	available (free)
der Gang (am Gang)	aisle (on the aisle)

119

das Gepäck	baggage
die Halle	terminal
das Handgepäck	hand luggage
der Inlandflug	domestic flight
der Koffer	suitcase
der Passagier	passenger
passen	to fit
der Platz	seat, place
rauchen	to smoke
die Reihe	row
die Reise	trip
reisen	to travel
der Reisepass	passport
der Schalter	counter
der Sitz	seat
sich verspäten	to be late
das Visum	visa
zeigen	to show

At the train station
Im Bahnhof

abfahren	to depart
die Abfahrt	departure
das Abteil	compartment
ankommen	to arrive
die Ankunft	arrival
aussteigen	to get off
der Bahnsteig	platform
bekommen	to get, receive
bezahlen	to pay
die einfache Fahrkarte	one-way ticket
einsteigen	to get on, board
der Fahrplan	schedule, timetable
der Gepäckträger	porter
das Gleis	track
der Liegewagen	sleeping car
die Platzreservierung	seat reservation

pünktlich	on time
die Rückfahrkarte	round-trip ticket
rufen	to call
der Schaffner	conductor
der Schlafwagen	sleeping car
der Speisewagen	dining car
tragen	to carry
umsteigen	to change trains
die Verspätung	delay
der Wagen	car
der Zug	train
der Zuschlag	supplement (to a ticket)

Asking for directions
Nach dem Weg fragen

abbiegen	to turn off
die Ampel	traffic light
die Autobahn	turnpike
die Auffahrt	entrance
die Abfahrt	exit
die Bundesstrasse	highway
die Ecke	corner
die Einbahnstrasse	one-way street
entfernt	far
folgen	to follow
zu Fuss gehen	to walk
geradeaus	straight ahead
die Haltestelle	stop (bus, etc.)
die Kreuzung	intersection
links	left
links um die Ecke	left around the corner
nach links fahren (gehen)	turn left
in der Nähe	near, in the vicinity
der Rastplatz	rest (picnic) area
die Raststätte	rest stop (with snack bar and gas)
rechts	right

die Richtung	direction
die Strasse	street, block
der Verkehr	traffic
der Vorort	outskirts
weit	far

A telephone call
Ein Telefongespräch

abheben, abnehmen	to pick up (receiver)
das Amt	bureau, office
der Anruf	telephone call
anrufen	to call up
der Anschluss	connection
auflegen	to hang up
ausser Betrieb	out of order
benutzen	to use
besetzt	busy
durchwählen	to dial directly
das Ferngespräch	long-distance call
der Hörer	receiver
das Kleingeld	small change
klingeln	to ring
die Nachricht	message
öffentlich	public
der Ort	town
das R-Gespräch	collect call
schauen	to look
telefonieren	to call up
unterbrechen	to cut off
verbinden	to connect
die Verbindung	connection
die Vorwahl	area code
wählen	to dial
warten	to wait

At the hotel
Im Hotel

ankommen	to arrive
anrechnen	to charge
anschalten	to turn on (light)
ausfüllen	to fill out
das Badezimmer	bathroom
die Bedienung	service
die Bestätigung	confirmation
bestellen	to reserve, to order
das Bett	bed
bieten	to offer
bleiben	to stay
die Decke	blanket
das Doppelbett	double bed
die Dusche	shower
das Einzelzimmer	single room
der Empfang (die Rezeption)	reception desk
das Frühstück	breakfast
der Gast	guest
die Halbpension	room with lunch or dinner
(im Preis) inbegriffen	included (in the price)
kalt	cold
mir ist kalt	I'm cold
das Kopfkissen	pillow
das Licht	light
die Rechnung	bill, total
reservieren	to reserve
die Sachen	things
der Schlüssel	key
die Seife	soap
übernachten	to stay overnight
unterschreiben	to sign
verlangen	to ask for
verlassen	to leave

die Vollpension	room and board
waschen	to wash
das Zimmer	room
Zimmer frei	room(s) available

At the bank
Auf der Bank

---

abheben	to withdraw, take out money
die Bank	bank

der (die) Bankangestellte	teller, bank employee
das Bargeld	cash
bezahlen	to pay for
das Darlehen	loan
einlösen	to cash (a check)
einzahlen	to deposit
erhalten	to receive
eröffnen	to open
das Geld	money
das Girokonto	checking account
die Hypothek	mortgage
die Kasse	cashier's window
das Konto	account
der Kontostand	balance
der Reisescheck	traveler's check
der Schein	bill (money)
sparen	to save
wachsen	to grow
der Wechselkurs	exchange rate
wechseln	to exchange, change
die Zinsen	interest

At the post office
Auf der Post

abholen	to pick up
abschicken	to send off, mail
die Adresse	address
der Brief	letter
die Briefmarke	stamp
der Briefumschlag	envelope
der Empfänger	receiver, addressee
der Kasten	box
die Luftpost	airmail
per Luftpost	via airmail
das Paket	package
die Post	mail
das Postamt	post office
die Postkarte	postcard
die Postleitzahl	zip code
schicken	to send
werfen	to throw
die Zollerklärung	customs declaration

At the clothing store
Im Kaufhaus

der Anzug	man's suit
der Badeanzug	bathing suit
die Baumwolle	cotton
die Bluse	blouse
der Büstenhalter (BH)	brassiere
empfehlen	to recommend
eng	narrow, tight
das Gewebe	fabric
die Grösse	size
der Gürtel	belt

die Handtasche	handbag
das Hemd	shirt
die Hose	pants
die Jacke	jacket (sports)
die Jeans	(blue) jeans
das Kleid	dress
der Knopf	button
die Krawatte	necktie
kurz	short
lang	long
das Leder	leather
der Mantel	coat
das Paar	pair
der Pullover (der Pulli)	pullover sweater
der Regenmantel	raincoat
der Reissverschluss	zipper
der Rock	skirt
der Schal	scarf
die Schuhe	shoes
der Stoff	material
die Stiefel	boots
die Unterwäsche	underclothes
vorziehen	to prefer

At the dry cleaner (laundry)
In der Reinigung (Wäscherei)

bügeln	to iron
einlaufen	to shrink
fertig	ready
der Fleck	stain
das Futter	lining
das Kleidungsstück	piece of clothing
der Knopf	button
das Loch	hole
nähen	to sew
reinigen	to dry-clean
reparieren	to repair, mend

schmutzig	dirty
der Schneider	tailor
die Stärke	starch
die Wäsche	wash, dirty laundry
waschen	to wash

At the Restaurant
Im Restaurant

---

die Bedienung	service
das Besteck	silverware
der Braten	roast
draussen	outside
durchgebraten	well done
der Durst	thirst
die Ecke	corner
englisch	rare (meat)
fehlen	to be missing
das Fenster	window
das Fleisch	meat
die Frucht	fruit
die Gabel	fork
der Garten	garden
die Gaststätte	restaurant
das Gedeck	place setting
das Geflügel	poultry
das Gemüse	vegetables
das Gericht	dish, course
das Getränk	drink
das Hauptgericht	main course
hungrig	hungry
inbegriffen	included
der Käse	cheese
der Kellner (die Kellnerin)	waiter (waitress)
der Löffel	spoon
das Menü	fixed menu
das Messer	knife

die Nachspeise	dessert
der Ober	waiter
der Pfeffer	pepper
probieren	to try, to taste
die Quittung	receipt
der Saft	juice
die Sahne	cream
der Salat	salad
das Salz	salt
schmecken	to taste (good)
schneiden	to cut
die Serviette	napkin
die Speise	food
die Speisekarte	menu
die Tageskarte	menu (of daily specials)
die Tasse	cup
der Teller	plate
teuer	expensive
der Tisch	table
die Tischdecke	tablecloth
die Vorspeise	appetizer
wünschen	to wish
zäh	tough
Zahlen, bitte!	Bill, please! (We'd like to pay)
der Zucker	sugar

At home
Zu Hause

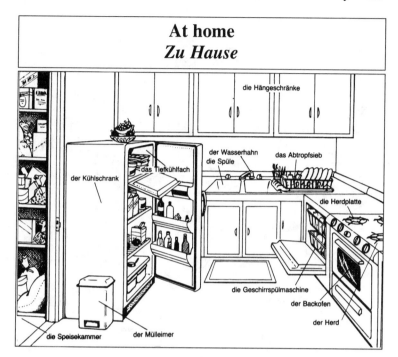

KITCHEN (*die Küche*)

die Abfälle	garbage
abtrocknen	to dry
aufdrehen	to turn on
braten	to fry, roast
die Dose	can
das Geschirr	dishes
der Herd	stove
kochen	to cook; to boil
der Kühlschrank	refrigerator
der Ofen	oven
schlagen	to beat
schliessen	to close
schneiden	to cut, carve
vorbereiten	to prepare

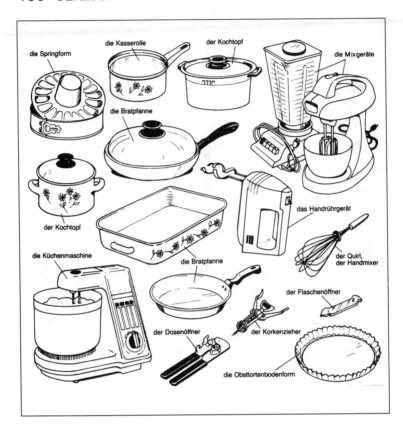

DINING ROOM (*das Esszimmer*)

abräumen	to clear the table
den Tisch decken	to set the table
das Glas	glass
die Mahlzeit	meal
Platz nehmen	to take a seat
reichen	to reach, to hand, to pass
die Serviette	napkin
stellen	to put
die Tasse	cup

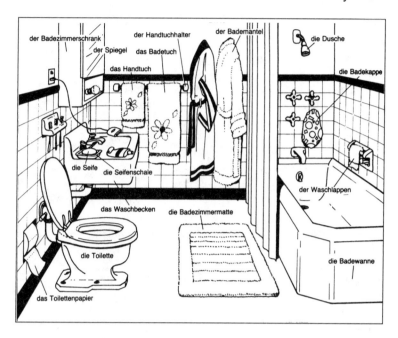

BATHROOM (*das Badezimmer*)

sich abtrocknen	to dry oneself
(sich) baden	to bathe
(sich) duschen	to shower
sich kämmen	to comb one's hair
nass	wet
sich die Zähne putzen	to brush one's teeth
der Rasierapparat	electric razor
sich rasieren	to shave
sich schminken	to apply makeup
sich waschen	to wash oneself
die Zahnbürste	toothbrush
die Zahnpaste	toothpaste

LIVING ROOM (*das Wohnzimmer*)

sich anhören	to listen to
bedecken	to cover
das Bild	picture

fernsehen	to watch television
der Fussboden	floor
die Lampe	lamp
das Radio	radio
der Teppich	carpet
sich unterhalten	to converse
die Zeitschrift	magazine
die Zeitung	newspaper

BEDROOM (*das Schlafzimmer*)

aufstehen	to get up
das Bett	bed
ins Bett gehen	to go to bed
einschlafen	to fall asleep
die Kommode	bureau
das Kopfkissen	(bed) pillow
die Matratze	mattress
schlafen	to sleep
der Schrank	closet
(den Wecker) stellen	to set (the alarm clock)
der Wecker	alarm clock

HOUSEWORK (*die Hausarbeit*)

das Bügeleisen	iron
kehren	to sweep
leeren	to empty
der Müll	garbage
der Mülleimer	garbage can
putzen	to clean
der Staub	dust
der Staubsauger	vacuum cleaner
staubsaugen	to vacuum
die Waschmaschine	washing machine
werfen	to throw
wischen	to wash (floor), wipe

At the doctor's office
Beim Arzt

der Arzt	doctor
die Ärztin	female doctor
das Bein	leg
die Beschwerden	complaints
das Blut	blood
der Blutdruck	blood pressure
die Blutgruppe	blood type
der Bruch	break, fracture
die Brust	chest; breast
der Darm	bowels, intestine
der Durchfall	diarrhea

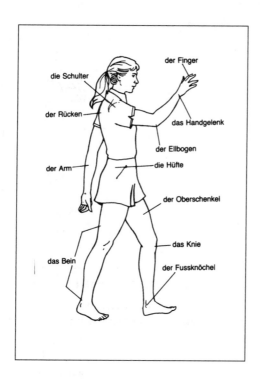

empfindlich gegen	sensitive to
entfernen	to remove
die Erkältung	cold
das Fieber	fever
der Fuss	foot
gebrochen	broken
das Herz	heart
husten	to cough
der Knochen	bone
die Kopfschmerzen	headache
krank	sick, ill
die Krankheit	sickness, illness
der Krebs	cancer
die Lungen	lungs
der Magen	stomach
der Mund	mouth
das Ohr	ear
das Pflaster	adhesive bandage
der Schlaganfall	stroke
die Schmerzen	pains
schwindelig	dizzy
die Spritze	injection
der Stuhl	stool
der Stuhlgang	bowel movement
die Symptome	symptoms
der Unfall	accident
untersuchen	to examine, analyze
verstopft	constipated
die Wange	cheek
weh tun	to hurt
die Wunde	wound

At the hospital
Im Krankenhaus

der Arzt/die Ärztin	doctor
atmen	to breathe
die Aufnahme	admission

die Bauchschmerzen	stomach pains, bellyache
bereit	ready
die Blase	bladder
der Blinddarm	appendix
der Chirurg, die Chirurgin	surgeon
die Entbindung	delivery
ernst	serious
das Formular	form (to fill out)
das Geschwür	ulcer
herausnehmen	to take out
die Krankenkasse	health insurance
der (die) Krankenpfleger(in)	nurse
die Krankenschwester	nurse (female)
die Mandeln	tonsils
die Operation	operation
der (die) Patient(in)	patient
der Puls	pulse
der Rollstuhl	wheelchair
die Röntgenbilder	x-rays
der Sauerstoff	oxygen
die Schmerzen	pains
schwanger	pregnant
die Spritze	injection
die Tragbahre	stretcher

At the theater and the movies
Im Theater und im Kino

anfangen	to begin
die Aufführung	performance
ausverkauft	sold out
die Bühne	stage
einen Film drehen	to shoot a film
(auf der Bühne) erscheinen	to appear (on stage)
fallen	to fall
die Garderobe	coatroom
der Held (die Heldin)	hero (heroine)
die Karte	ticket

das Kino	movies, cinema
die Komödie	comedy
die Leinwand	screen
die Pause	intermission
der Platz	seat
die Reihe	row
die Rolle	part, role
das Schauspiel	play
der Schauspieler (die Schauspielerin)	actor (actress)
eine Rolle spielen	to act, to play a part
das Theater	theater
der Vorhang	curtain
die Vorstellung	show, performance
vorziehen	to prefer
zeigen	to show, to present
der Zuschauer	spectator

Sports
Der Sport

abfahren	to ski down
der Abfahrtslauf	downhill skiing
die Alpinskier	alpine skis
der Anfänger	beginner
anhalten	to stop
der Ball	ball
benutzen	to use
die Berge	mountains
die Bindungen	bindings
das Bremsen	braking
das Doppel	doubles match (tennis)
einstellen	to adjust
fangen	to catch
das Fussballfeld	soccer field
die Fussballmannschaft	soccer team
gewinnen	to win
gleiten	to glide

die Handschuhe	gloves
der Langlauf	cross-country skiing
die Langlaufskier	Nordic skis
das Netz	net
pfeifen	to whistle
die Piste	ski slope, run
der Punkt	point
die Saison	season
der Satz	set (tennis)
der Schiedsrichter	referee
der Schnee	snow
schwer	difficult
das Skifahren	skiing
die Spieler	players
der Tennisplatz	tennis court
das Tor	goal
ein Tor schiessen	to score a goal
der Torwart	goal tender
unentschieden	tied
verloren	lost
zurückschlagen	to return (the ball)

At the beach
Am Strand

der Badeanzug	bathing suit
die Badehose	bathing trunks
baden	to bathe, swim
bekannt	well known
das Boot	boat
braun werden	to tan
die Ebbe	low tide
die Flut	high tide
gefährlich	dangerous
die Haut	skin
die Luftmatratze	air mattress
das Meer, die See	sea
der Rettungsschwimmer	lifeguard

ruhig	calm
der Sand	sand
schwimmen	to swim
das Segelboot	sailboat
der Sonnenbrand	sunburn
die Sonnenbrille	sunglasses
das Sonnenöl	suntan lotion
der Strand	beach, shore
der Urlaub	vacation (adults)
Urlaub machen	to vacation
wandern	to wander, hike
Wasserski laufen	to water-ski
die Welle	wave
windsurfen	to windsurf

Camping
Wir campen

der Anhänger	trailer
anzünden	to light (a fire)
campen	to camp
der Campingplatz	campsite
das Lagerfeuer	campfire, bonfire
der Rucksack	knapsack, backpack
der Schlafsack	sleeping bag
das Streichholz	match
die Taschenlampe	flashlight
das Taschenmesser	penknife
die Thermosflasche	thermos bottle
das Trinkwasser	drinking water
der Verbandskasten	first aid kit
der Wasserkanister	canteen (water canister)
das Zelt	tent
ein Zelt aufstellen	to pitch a tent
die Zeltstange	tent pole
zubereiten	to prepare

The weather
Das Wetter

angenehm	pleasant
die Aussichten	outlook (weather)
bewölkt	cloudy
der Blitz	lightning
blitzen	to lighten
der Donner	thunder
donnern	to thunder
feucht	humid
die Feuchtigkeit	humidity
das Gewitter	thunderstorm
der Hagel	hail
heiss	hot
der Himmel	sky
die Höchsttemperatur	maximum temperature
klar	clear
der Luftdruck	barometric pressure
manchmal	sometimes
der Nebel	fog
der Niederschlag	precipitation
der Regen	rain
regnen	to rain
regnerisch	rainy
die Richtung	direction
scheinen	to shine
der Schnee	snow
schneien	to snow
die Sonne	sun
sonnig	sunny
stark	strong
steigen	to rise
der Sturm	storm
stürmisch	stormy
die Temperatur	temperature
die Tiefsttemperatur	minimum temperature

überwiegend	predominant
warm	warm
wechselnd	changing
das Wetter	weather
der Wetterbericht	weather report
die Wettervorhersage	weather prediction
windig	windy
die Wolke	cloud
wolkig	cloudy

Education
Das Bildungswesen

das Abitur	diploma (secondary school)
bestehen	to pass a test
besuchen	to attend (school)
das Buch	book
der (die) Dekan(in)	dean
der Doktorgrad	doctorate
durchfallen	to fail
sich einschreiben	to register
das Fach	subject
die Fakultät	school (of medicine, law, philosophy, etc.)
der (die) Gasthörer(in)	auditor
die Grundschule	elementary school
die Hochschule	university (technical)
sich immatrikulieren	to matriculate
die Klasse	class
das Klassenzimmer	classroom
der Kugelschreiber	ball-point pen
lehren	to teach
lernen	to learn
lesen	to read
die Note	grade, mark
die Prüfung	test, examination
eine Prüfung ablegen	to take a test

das Pult	desk
der Rektor	principal
die Schule	school
das Studentenwohnheim	dormitory
die Studiengebühr	tuition
studieren	to study; to attend a university; to major in
die Universität	university
unterrichten	to teach
die Vorlesung	lecture
das Zeugnis	report card

The state and politics
Staat und Politik

der (die) Abgeordnete	representative
abstimmen	to vote
die Abstimmung	vote
ändern	to change, amend
der Ausschuss	committee
sich beraten (über)	to deliberate (about)
bestimmen	to determine
der Bundeskanzler	chancellor (federal)
das Bundesland	federal state (Germany)
der Bundesrat	German upper house
der Bundestag	German lower house
der Bürger	citizen
der Diktator	dictator
die Diktatur	dictatorship
die Koalition	coalition
das Land	country
die Mehrheit	majority
die Menschenrechte	human rights
der Ministerpräsident	president of the cabinet council
die Partei	political party
die Politik	policies, politics
die Regierung	government

der Staat	state
die Stimme	voice, vote
stimmen für	to vote for
die Verfassung	constitution
vertreten	to represent
das Volk	people
wählen	to vote

The automobile
Das Auto

der Abschleppwagen	tow truck
die Batterie	battery
das Benzin	gasoline
bremsen	to brake
einstellen	to adjust
der Ersatzreifen	spare tire
die Ersatzteile	spare parts
der Führerschein	driver's license
der Gang	gear
im ersten Gang	in first gear
die Handbremse	hand brake
das Handschuhfach	glove compartment
die Hupe	horn
das Kennzeichen	license plate
der Kilometerzähler	odometer (kilometers)
klopfen	to knock
der Kofferraum	trunk
der Kühler	radiator
kuppeln	to clutch or to (engage the) clutch
leer	empty
das Lenkrad	steering wheel
mieten	to rent
das Öl	oil
der Ölstand	oil level
die Panne	breakdown

einen Platten haben	to have a flat tire
der Reifen	tire
schalten	to shift (gears)
die Stossstange	bumper
die Tankstelle	gas station
der Unfall	accident
der Verkehr	traffic
der Wagen	car
die Zündkerze	spark plug

Appendix
VERB CHART

Principal Parts of Verbs

Below is a list of the most commonly used strong and irregular verbs.

Infinitive	Simple Past	Past Participle	Present Stem	English
backen	backte (old: buk)	gebacken	bäckt	to bake
beginnen	begann	begonnen		to begin
beißen	biß	gebissen		to bite
biegen	bog	gebogen		to bend
binden	band	gebunden		to bind
bitten	bat	gebeten		to ask
bleiben	blieb	ist geblieben		to stay
brechen	brach	gebrochen	bricht	to break
brennen	brannte	gebrannt		to burn
bringen	brachte	gebracht		to bring
denken	dachte	gedacht		to think
dürfen	durfte	gedurft	darf	to be allowed
essen	aß	gegessen	ißt	to eat
fahren	fuhr	gefahren	fährt	to go, drive
fallen	fiel	ist gefallen	fällt	to fall
fangen	fing	gefangen	fängt	to catch
finden	fand	gefunden		to find
fliegen	flog	ist geflogen		to fly
fliehen	floh	ist geflohen		to flee

fließen	floß	ist geflossen		to flow
fressen	fraß	gefressen	frißt	to eat (of animals)
frieren	fror	gefroren		to freeze, be cold
geben	gab	gegeben	gibt	to give
gehen	ging	ist gegangen		to go
gewinnen	gewann	gewonnen		to win
graben	grub	gegraben	gräbt	to dig
haben	hatte	gehabt	hat	to have
halten	hielt	gehalten	hält	to hold, stop
helfen	half	geholfen	hilft	to help
kennen	kannte	gekannt		to know
kommen	kam	ist gekommen		to come
können	konnte	gekonnt	kann	can, to be able
lassen	ließ	gelassen	läßt	to let, leave
laufen	lief	ist gelaufen	läuft	to run, walk
leiden	litt	gelitten		to suffer
leihen	lieh	geliehen		to loan
lesen	las	gelesen	liest	to read
liegen	lag	gelegen		to lie
messen	maß	gemessen	mißt	to measure
mögen	mochte	gemocht	mag	to like
müssen	mußte	gemußt	muß	must, to have to
nehmen	nahm	genommen	nimmt	to take
nennen	nannte	genannt		to name, call
reiten	ritt	ist geritten		to ride
rennen	rannte	ist gerannt		to run
riechen	roch	gerochen		to smell
saufen	soff	gesoffen	säuft	to drink (of animals)
scheinen	schien	geschienen		to shine, seem
schießen	schoß	geschossen		to shoot
schlafen	schlief	geschlafen	schläft	to sleep
schlagen	schlug	geschlagen	schlägt	to hit
schließen	schloß	geschlossen		to close

schneiden	schnitt	geschnitten		to cut
schreiben	schrieb	geschrieben		to write
schreien	schrie	geschrien		to scream
schweigen	schwieg	geschwiegen		to be silent
schwimmen	schwamm	ist geschwommen		to swim
sehen	sah	gesehen	sieht	to see
sein	war	ist gewesen	ist	to be
senden	sandte	gesandt		to send
singen	sang	gesungen		to sing
sinken	sank	gesunken		to sink
sitzen	saß	gesessen		to sit
sollen	sollte	gesollt	soll	ought, to be supposed to
sprechen	sprach	gesprochen	spricht	to speak
springen	sprang	ist gesprungen		to jump
stehen	stand	gestanden		to stand
stehlen	stahl	gestohlen	stiehlt	to steal
steigen	stieg	ist gestiegen		to climb
sterben	starb	ist gestorben	stirbt	to die
stinken	stank	gestunken		to stink
tragen	trug	getragen	trägt	to wear, carry
treffen	traf	getroffen	trifft	to meet
treten	trat	ist getreten	tritt	to step
trinken	trank	getrunken		to drink
tun	tat	getan		to do
verlieren	verlor	verloren		to lose
wachsen	wuchs	ist gewachsen	wächst	to grow
waschen	wusch	gewaschen	wäscht	to wash
wenden	wandte	gewandt		to turn
werden	wurde	ist geworden	wird	to become
werfen	warf	geworfen	wirft	to throw
wiegen	wog	gewogen		to weigh
wissen	wußte	gewußt	weiß	to know
wollen	wollte	gewollt	will	to want to
ziehen	zog	gezogen		to pull

Index

147